W9-BHR-161

JEAN CRAIGHEAD GEORGE

One Day in the Tropical Rain Forest

ILLUSTRATED BY GARY ALLEN

Here's all the great literature in this grade level of *Celebrate Reading!*

NUMBER THE STARS

CLASS PRESIDENT

MARY POPPINS

REVISED EDITION

P. L. TRAVERS

Flights of Fancy
Journeys of the Imagination

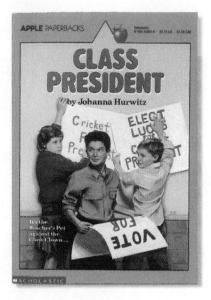

Before Your Very Eyes

A World of Nature

Featured Poets
Marilyn Singer
Byrd Baylor
George David Weiss
Bob Thiele

Many People, Many Voices
Stories of America

Featured Poets
Duke Redbird
Linh To Sinh My Bui

Within My Reach

The Important Things in Life

Handle with Care

Making a Difference

All About Sam
from the novel by Lois Lowry
✷ Mark Twain Award

Number the Stars
from the novel by Lois Lowry
✷ Newbery Medal
✷ ALA Notable Children's Book
✷ Teachers' Choice
✷ Notable Social Studies Trade Book

Jessi's Secret Language
from the novel by Ann M. Martin

Take a Walk in Their Shoes
from the biography by
Glennette Tilley Turner
✷ Notable Social Studies Trade Book

Dorothea Lange: Life Through the Camera
from the biography by
Milton Meltzer
✷ Boston Globe-Horn Book
Award Author

Featured Poets
Ouida Sebestyen
Danny Williams

Ask Me Again Tomorrow

Growing and Changing

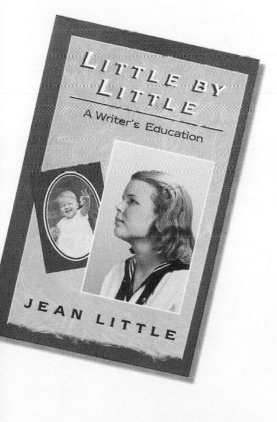

ASK ME AGAIN TOMORROW

GROWING AND CHANGING

Cover Story
José Cruz is the artist responsible for creating the
Mood-O-Meter on the cover of *Ask Me Again
Tomorrow*. Mr. Cruz's style, which he calls
"geometrix," is half geometry, giving his art the three
dimensional quality often missing in illustration.

ISBN 0-673-80056-3

Acknowledgments appear on page 144.

5678910RRS999897969594

ASK ME AGAIN TOMORROW

MOOD-O-METER

GROWING AND CHANGING

ScottForesman

A Division of HarperCollins*Publishers*

CONTENTS

I'm a Different Person Now!

Large Enough for All of Us

F·6

by Gary Soto

anuel was the fourth of seven children and looked like a lot of kids in his neighborhood: black hair, brown face, and skinny legs scuffed from summer play. But summer was giving way to fall: the trees were turning red, the lawns brown, and the pomegranate trees were heavy with fruit. Manuel walked to school in the frosty morning, kicking leaves and thinking of tomorrow's talent show. He was still amazed that he had volunteered. He was going to pretend to sing Ritchie Valens's "La Bamba" before the entire school.

hy did I raise my hand? he asked himself, but in his heart he knew the answer.

He yearned for the limelight. He wanted applause as loud as a thunderstorm, and to hear his friends say, "Man, that was bad!" And he wanted to impress the girls, especially Petra Lopez, the second-prettiest girl in his class. The prettiest was already taken by his friend Ernie. Manuel knew he should be reasonable, since he himself was not great-looking, just average.

Manuel kicked through the fresh-fallen leaves. When he got to school he realized he had forgotten his math workbook. If the teacher found out, he would have to stay after school and miss practice for the talent show. But fortunately for him, they did drills that morning.

During lunch Manuel hung around with Benny, who was also in the talent show. Benny was going to play the trumpet in spite of the fat lip he had gotten playing football.

"How do I look?" Manuel asked. He cleared his throat and started moving his lips in pantomime. No words came out, just a hiss that sounded like a snake. Manuel tried to look emotional, flailing his arms on the high notes and opening his eyes and mouth as wide as he could when he came to *"Para bailar la baaaaammmba."*

After Manuel finished, Benny said it looked all right, but suggested Manuel dance while he sang. Manuel thought for a moment and decided it was a good idea.

"Yeah, just think you're like Michael Jackson or someone like that," Benny suggested. "But don't get carried away."

During rehearsal, Mr. Roybal, nervous about his debut as the school's talent coordinator, cursed under his breath when the lever that controlled the speed on the record player jammed.

"Darn," he growled, trying to force the lever. "What's wrong with you?"

"Is it broken?" Manuel asked, bending over for a closer look. It looked all right to him.

Mr. Roybal assured Manuel that he would have a good record player at the talent show, even if it meant bringing his own stereo from home.

*M*anuel sat in a folding chair, twirling his record on his thumb. He watched a skit about personal hygiene, a mother-and-daughter violin duo, five first-grade girls jumping rope, a karate kid breaking boards, three girls singing "Like a Virgin," and a skit about the pilgrims. If the record player hadn't been broken, he would have gone after the karate kid, an easy act to follow, he told himself.

As he twirled his forty-five record, Manuel thought they had a great talent show. The entire school would be amazed. His mother and father would be proud, and his brothers and sisters would be jealous and pout. It would be a night to remember.

Benny walked onto the stage, raised his trumpet to his mouth, and waited for his cue. Mr. Roybal raised his hand like a symphony conductor and let it fall dramatically. Benny inhaled and blew so loud that Manuel dropped his record, which rolled across the cafeteria floor until it hit a wall. Manuel raced after it, picked it up, and wiped it clean.

"Boy, I'm glad it didn't break," he said with a sigh.

hat night Manuel had to do the dishes and a lot of homework, so he could only practice in the shower. In bed he prayed that he wouldn't mess up. He prayed that it wouldn't be like when he was a

first-grader. For Science Week he had wired together a
C battery and a bulb, and told everyone he had
discovered how a flashlight worked. He was so pleased
with himself that he practiced for hours pressing the wire
to the battery, making the bulb wink a dim, orangish
light. He showed it to so many kids in his neighborhood
that when it was time to show his class how a flashlight
worked, the battery was dead. He pressed the wire to the
battery, but the bulb didn't respond. He pressed until his
thumb hurt and some kids in the back started snickering.

But Manuel fell asleep confident that nothing would
go wrong this time.

The next morning his father and mother beamed at

him. They were proud that he was going to be in the talent show.

"I wish you would tell us what you're doing," his mother said. His father, a pharmacist who wore a blue smock with his name on a plastic rectangle, looked up from the newspaper and sided with his wife. "Yes, what are you doing in the talent show?"

"You'll see," Manuel said with his mouth full of Cheerios.

The day whizzed by, and so did his afternoon chores and dinner. Suddenly he was dressed in his best clothes and standing next to Benny backstage, listening to the commotion as the cafeteria filled with school kids and parents. The lights dimmed, and Mr. Roybal, sweaty in a tight suit and a necktie with a large knot, wet his lips and parted the stage curtains.

"Good evening, everyone," the kids behind the curtain heard him say. "Good evening to you," some of the smart-alecky kids said back to him.

"Tonight we bring you the best John Burroughs Elementary has to offer, and I'm sure that you'll be both pleased and amazed that our little school houses so much talent. And now, without further ado, let's get on with the show." He turned and, with a swish of his hand, commanded, "Part the curtain." The curtains parted in jerks. A girl dressed as a toothbrush and a boy dressed as a dirty gray tooth walked onto the stage and sang:

Brush, brush, brush
Floss, floss, floss
Gargle the germs away—hey! hey! hey!

fter they finished singing, they turned to Mr. Roybal, who dropped his hand. The toothbrush dashed around the stage after the dirty tooth, which was laughing and having a great time until it slipped and nearly rolled off the stage.

Mr. Roybal jumped out and caught it just in time. "Are you OK?"

The dirty tooth answered, "Ask my dentist," which drew laughter and applause from the audience.

The violin duo played next, and except for one time when the girl got lost, they sounded fine. People applauded, and some even stood up. Then the first-grade girls maneuvered onto the stage while jumping rope. They were all smiles and bouncing ponytails as a hundred cameras flashed at once. Mothers "awhed" and fathers sat up proudly.

The karate kid was next. He did a few kicks, yells, and chops, and finally, when his father held up a board, punched it in two. The audience clapped and looked at each other, wide-eyed with respect. The boy bowed to the audience, and father and son ran off the stage.

Manuel remained behind the stage shivering with fear.

He mouthed the words to "La Bamba" and swayed from left to right. Why did he raise his hand and volunteer? Why couldn't he have just sat there like the rest of the kids and not said anything? While the karate kid was on stage, Mr. Roybal, more sweaty than before, took Manuel's forty-five record and placed it on a new record player.

"You ready?" Mr. Roybal asked.

"Yeah . . ."

Mr. Roybal walked back on stage and announced that Manuel Gomez, a fifth-grader in Mrs. Knight's class, was going to pantomime Ritchie Valens's classic hit "La Bamba."

The cafeteria roared with applause. Manuel was nervous but loved the noisy crowd. He pictured his mother and father applauding loudly and his brothers and sister also clapping, though not as energetically.

anuel walked on stage and the song started immediately. Glassy-eyed from the shock of being in front of so many people, Manuel moved his lips and swayed in a made-up dance step. He couldn't see his parents, but he could see his brother Mario, who was a year younger, thumb-wrestling with a friend. Mario was wearing Manuel's favorite shirt; he would deal with Mario later. He saw some other kids get up and head for the drinking fountain, and a baby sitting

F·15

in the middle of an aisle sucking her thumb and watching him intently.

What am I doing here? thought Manuel. This is no fun at all. Everyone was just sitting there. Some people were moving to the beat, but most were just watching him, like they would a monkey at the zoo.

But when Manuel did a fancy dance step, there was a burst of applause and some girls screamed. Manuel tried another dance step. He heard more applause and screams and started getting into the groove as he shivered and snaked like Michael Jackson around the stage. But the record got stuck, and he had to sing

Para bailar la bamba
Para bailar la bamba
Para bailar la bamba
Para bailar la bamba

again and again.

Manuel couldn't believe his bad luck. The audience began to laugh and stand up in their chairs. Manuel remembered how the forty-five record had dropped from his hand and rolled across the cafeteria floor. It probably got scratched, he thought, and now it was stuck, and he was stuck dancing and moving his lips to the same words over and over. He had never been so embarrassed. He would have to ask his parents to move the family out of town.

After Mr. Roybal ripped the needle across the record, Manuel slowed his dance steps to a halt. He didn't know what to do except bow to the audience, which applauded wildly, and scoot off the stage, on the verge of tears. This was worse than the homemade flashlight. At least no one laughed then, they just snickered.

anuel stood alone, trying hard to hold back the tears as Benny, center stage, played his trumpet. Manuel was jealous because he sounded great, then mad as he recalled that it was Benny's loud trumpet playing that made the forty-five record fly out of his hands. But when the entire cast lined up for a curtain call, Manuel received a burst of applause that was so loud it shook the walls of the cafeteria. Later, as he mingled with the kids and parents, everyone patted him on the shoulder and told him, "Way to go. You were really funny."

Funny? Manuel thought. Did he do something funny?

Funny. Crazy. Hilarious. These were the words people said to him. He was confused, but beyond caring. All he knew was that people were paying attention to him, and his brother and sisters looked at him with a mixture of jealousy and awe. He was going to pull Mario aside and punch him in the arm for wearing his shirt, but he cooled it. He was enjoying the limelight. A teacher brought him cookies and punch, and the popular kids who had never before given him the time of day now clustered around him. Ricardo, the editor of the school bulletin, asked him how he made the needle stick.

"It just happened," Manuel said, crunching on a star-shaped cookie.

At home that night his father, eager to undo the buttons on his shirt and ease into his La-Z-Boy recliner, asked Manuel the same thing, how he managed to make the song stick on the words *"Para bailar la bamba."*

Manuel thought quickly and reached for scientific jargon he had read in magazines. "Easy, Dad. I used laser tracking with high optics and low functional decibels per channel." His proud but confused father told him to be quiet and go to bed.

"Ah, que niños tan truchas," he said as he walked to the kitchen for a glass of milk. "I don't know how you kids nowadays get so smart."

Manuel, feeling happy, went to his bedroom, undressed, and slipped into his pajamas. He looked in the mirror and began to pantomime "La Bamba," but stopped because he was tired of the song. He crawled into bed. The sheets were as cold as the moon that stood over the peach tree in their backyard.

He was relieved that the day was over. Next year, when they asked for volunteers for the talent show, he wouldn't raise his hand. Probably.

1　Does this story remind you of a school program you've seen or been part of? Does it remind you of your own experiences with stage fright? Tell about one or the other or both: school programs, stage fright.

2　In the last paragraph, Manuel makes a decision. Do you think he'll change his mind? Which parts of the story support your response?

3　You've been asked to participate in a talent show at school. What will your act be? Plan something unique.

F·20

EL CHINO

by ALLEN SAY

My parents came from Canton, China, and had six children in Nogales, Arizona. I was the fourth child. They named me Bong Way Wong, but my brothers and sisters called me Billy.

Our home was a corner grocery store, and we were open for business every day of the year.

"In America, you can be anything you want to be," Dad told us.

That was good news because none of us wanted to be a grocer when we grew up.

Lily, the eldest, was studying to be a librarian. Rose and Florence wanted to be teachers. My older brother, Jack, loved engineering. And Art, my baby brother, said he was going to be a doctor.

All I wanted to do was play basketball.

"Who's ever heard of a Chinese athlete!" They laughed.

They didn't understand. I wanted to be a *great* athlete.

"Why don't you listen to Dad," I told them.

But Dad died suddenly when I was ten. Our days were dark after that, and we had to be a stronger family than we were before. We gathered around Mom and went on with our business.

In high school I finally got to play serious basketball. I was quick and fast, and I could shoot from anywhere on the court. "My ace," the coach used to call me.

But I never got to play in college. I was too short.

"Just think," I said to my brother, Jack. "Four inches taller and I would've been famous!"

"Who's going to hire a Chinese ballplayer, anyway?" he asked. "Learn a trade and earn a living like everybody else."

So, like Jack, I studied engineering.

After college I got a job as a highway engineer. That made everybody happy, especially Mom.

But I kept thinking about shooting the winning basket with the clock running out.

"Give Billy the ball!" they used to yell.

And they always did. I'd spin and shoot all in one motion, and the whole gym would explode with my name.

"Billy! Billy! Billy!"

I never forgot that.

Give me the ball!

But by then I had a trade and earned a living. For my first vacation I went to Europe. I liked Spain best—it was hot there, like it was in Arizona. I saw castles and museums, cathedrals and Gypsy dancers.

Then I saw a bullfight.

It's a sport where the bullfighter fools the bull with a cloth cape and kills it with a sword. Sometimes the bull kills the bullfighter. It wasn't anything like the rodeo shows I'd seen back home.

The first time the bull charged the bullfighter, I closed my eyes.

"Olé!" The crowd screamed, and I paid attention.

It was a spectacle, all right, a very dangerous circus. And the bullfighter was some kind of an athlete. He was graceful, too, like a ballet dancer, and had the steadiest nerves I'd ever seen. The bull kept missing him, and with each miss the audience yelled louder. I shouted with them, until my voice was gone.

When the fight was over, the bull was dead. And now it was the people who charged the bullfighter. Roaring at the top of their voices, they hoisted him onto their shoulders and marched out of the arena. I rushed after them.

I didn't have to chase far. I even managed to stand right next to the amazing daredevil, and I got a shock. He was much shorter than me!

That night I didn't sleep. I couldn't get him to stop dancing inside my head, that short Spaniard in a fancy outfit.

In the morning, I bought myself some Spanish clothes. Then I got a room in a boarding house, where I put away my old clothes and put on the new. In the mirror, I looked like a fine Spanish gentleman.

Using my hands and arms, I asked the landlady, "Where is the bullfighting school?"

F·29

"Ah, Señor." She gazed at me with great pity in her eyes. "Only the Spaniards can become true matadors."

She sounded like my mother. And that reminded me to send Mom a telegram, and also one to my boss. Very sorry and please forgive, I am not coming home.

The school was just a clearing in a wood outside the city, but the maestro had been a famous matador when he was young. We took turns playing the bull, and the old master taught us to use the cape and the sword.

"He is a good athlete," I heard one student say about me.

"And he has courage and grace," said another. "But he cannot be a matador. He is not Spanish."

My dad would've said a few things to them, but it was no use. How could they understand? They hadn't grown up in the United States.

Before I knew, it was springtime in Spain. That's when the bull ranchers hired student matadors to test their young cows for courage and spirit. And the students who fought well would go on to become real matadors. Like my classmates, I went looking for work.

F·31

Everywhere I went, though, the ranchers took one look at me and shook their heads. My family sent me love and money, and that kept me going, but after two years I still hadn't fought a single cow. Maybe it was time to give up, time to go home and be an engineer again.

But what would Dad have said to me now?

I'd tell him this wasn't Arizona, U.S.A. So I couldn't be a Spanish matador.

But *un momento,* Señor. A Spanish matador? What had I been thinking all this time?

I'm Chinese!

I searched all over town, and finally found what I was looking for—a Chinese costume. I tried it on and hardly recognized myself in the mirror.

It was as if I were seeing myself for the first time. I looked like a *real* Chinese. And as I stared in the mirror, a strange feeling came over me. I felt powerful. I felt that I could do anything I wished—even become a matador! Could it be that I was wearing a magical costume?

I went outside to see what would happen.

I was a spectacle.

Children followed me everywhere I went. Men greeted me from across the street. Women smiled.

F·33

"El Chino!" they shouted. The Chinese!

For the first time, people were taking notice of me, and that was magic.

It was time to go see a bull rancher.

Sure enough, the first rancher I saw gave me the nod. Just like that, I was facing my first live bull.

Actually, it was only a heifer, but it looked more like a black rhino, with horns that could gore right through me.

"I will not back off," I said to myself, and waved the cape.

The black hulk stood still, swishing a tail like a lion's.

"*Ojo, toro-o-o!*" I called, giving the cape a good flap.

The charge was sudden and fast.

Like a tumbling boulder, the heifer came straight at me, and I swung the cape. At the last moment she swerved and went for the cape. *Swoosh!* With a hot wind she was past me. I spun around, flapped the cape, and she charged again. Then again.

I didn't remember how many passes I'd made before I heard the ranch hands shouting. They wanted to see how I would end the fight.

So I made her charge me one more time, and then I walked away without looking back, as I had seen real matadors do. I prayed the heifer wouldn't gore me in my back. She didn't move.

"Olé, olé!" The crowd applauded me. I'd passed the test.

The next morning a bald-headed man came knocking on my door.

"I hear good things about you, Señor," he said. "I am a manager of bullfighters. Do you want me to help you become a matador?"

"Sí!" I almost shouted. "I would be honored!"

"*Bueno.* But you cannot fight in your strange costume. Come with me," he said, and took me to a tailor's shop.

There, I was fitted for the "suit of lights," which all matadors wear in bullrings. I felt like a prince being groomed for an important ceremony.

And there *was* a ceremony. My manager had made an arrangement for me to fight a real bull in a month's time!

"You are a sensation," he told me. "The plaza is sold out, and it is El Chino everyone wants to see."

Finally it was my day.

In a short while my manager would be arriving with a lot of reporters and photographers. I was big news. And my manager was supposed to help me get into the "suit of lights," but I couldn't wait any longer and got into it on my own.

In the mirror I looked splendid.

"Good thing you weren't four inches taller," I said to myself. "Show them you have grace and courage like the best of them. Don't lose face, for your family's sake . . ."

As I stared in the mirror, I began to feel victorious already. There had never been a Chinese matador before me. I could almost hear the sold-out plaza cheering me on. And if I fought well, maybe a crowd of Spaniards would carry me out of the arena on their shoulders, shouting my name the whole time.

And that's the way it happened. Just as I had dreamed it. "Olé! El Chino, olé!"

F·39

A DREAM IN BRIGHT SUNLIGHT

by ALLEN SAY

First time I heard about Billy Wong was in 1967, the year he became a matador called El Chino. I was a hungry young artist then, and the story made a deep impression on me.

In those days, Asian American boys were expected to become gardeners and laundrymen, chop suey cooks and storekeepers—maybe engineers and even doctors if they were super smart.

But here was a Chinese bullfighter! The world had never seen one before. How did he get such a dream? How did he pursue it? I was more than curious because I had a big dream of my own. Ever since I was a small boy I wanted to be a famous artist, and I longed to see my dream in bright sunlight, as Billy did. I felt a kinship with him.

Billy Wong died in a car accident two years later. I went on chasing after my dream and soon thought no more about the Chinese matador.

Then in 1989, when my daughter was in second grade, I went to her school party and met a woman named Janet Wong. Her husband, Dr. Art Wong, turned out to be the baby brother of El Chino! When I heard this, I was overcome with a powerful urge to write a story about Billy Wong. I had no idea how I was going to do it. Would any publisher buy such a story? After all, bullfighting was—and is—as popular as whaling or bashing of baby seals. Still, I wanted to write about Billy. His dream was what interested me.

I interviewed Art Wong and two older sisters, Lily and Rose. I borrowed their family albums and scrapbooks and pored over them, but Billy Wong remained a stranger to me. I didn't know where his dream came from or what it meant. I couldn't start writing.

So I worked on the illustrations first, and a wonderful thing happened. I began to see through Billy's eyes. Not only that, I thought with his mind and felt with his heart. It was like what a great Chinese painter once said: "When you paint a tiger, you must become a bit of the tiger yourself."

The pictures took eleven months to complete. The story took two days to write. I simply told *my* story through Billy's mouth.

I was sixteen when I came to the United States. For a long time I felt both visible and invisible in this country—visible because I looked different; invisible because I didn't belong. This is what Billy meant when he put on his Chinese costume and said, "For the first time, people were taking notice of me, and that was magic." That's the author talking.

When the book was finally published, Billy's younger sister, Florence, wrote to thank me. She said, "He [Billy] lives." It's the greatest compliment an artist can receive. That was *my* day in the sun.

THINKING ABOUT IT

1   What kind of person is Billy? Does he remind you
    of anyone you know?

2   What would you ask Allen Say about his book?

3   You are staging a scene from this selection. What
    scene will you choose? Why? How will you make
    that scene interesting to an audience?

Another Book Illustrated by Allen Say
Allen Say beautifully illustrates *The Boy of the
Three-Year Nap,* a Japanese folk tale retold by Diane
Snyder.

WRITERS

by Jean Little

Emily writes of poetic things
Like crocuses and hummingbirds' wings,
But I think people beat hummingbirds every time.

Emily likes to write of snow
And dawn and candlelight aglow,
But I'd rather write about me and Emily and stuff like that.

The funny thing is, I delight
To read what Emily likes to write,
And Emily says she thinks my poems are okay too.

Also, sometimes, we switch with each other.
Emily writes of a fight with her mother.
I tell about walking alone by the river,
    —how still and golden it was.

I know what Emily means, you see,
And, often, Emily's halfway me. . . .
Oh, there's just no way to make anybody else understand.

We're not a bit the same and yet,
We're closer than most people get.
There's no one word for it. We just care about each other
   the way we are supposed to.

So I can look through Emily's eyes
And she through mine. It's no surprise,
When you come right down to it, that we're friends.

P·45

F·46

Memories of Fifth Grade

from *Little by Little:
A Writer's Education*

by Jean Little

I looked up from my grade five reader and smiled. I liked Miss Marr a lot. And, even though we had only met an hour ago, I thought she liked me, too.

She was young and pretty and she had a gentle voice. But that was not all. Like Mr. Johnston, she had had polio. As I listened to her passing out books behind me, I could hear her limping, first a quick step, then a slow one.

Jean Little, award-winning author of children's books, writes of the challenges she faced as the new girl in school.

The sound made me feel a little less lonely. My teacher would understand how it felt to be the only cross-eyed girl in Victory School.

"This is your desk, Jean," she had said.

It sat, all by itself, right up against the front blackboard. I was supposed to be able to see better there. I had not yet managed to make anyone understand that if I wanted to read what was written on the board, I would have to stand up so that my face was only inches away from the writing. Then I would have to walk back and forth, following the words not only with my eyes but with my entire body. If the writing were up at the top of the board, I would have to stand on tiptoe or even climb on a chair to be able to decipher it. If it were near the bottom, I would have to crouch down.

I remembered Miss Bogart printing large, thick, yellow letters on a green chalkboard. That had been so different. These dusty grey boards looked almost the same color as the thin, white scratches Miss Marr's chalk made. Her small, neat words were composed of letters that flowed into each other, too, which made reading them even harder.

I would not explain. How could I? She might make me climb and crouch to read the words.

I stood out far too much as it was. All the desks except mine were nailed to the floor in five straight rows. The seats flipped up when you slid out of them. They were attached to the desk behind. On top was a trough for your pencil and, in the right-hand corner, an inkwell which Miss Marr kept filled from a big ink bottle with a long spout. All the desk lids were a dark wine color.

My desk was new and varnished a shiny golden brown. It had been provided for me because, in theory, it could be moved to wherever I could see best. It was, however, far too heavy and unwieldy for Miss Marr or me to shift. All that special desk did was single me out even more.

I turned sideways in my new desk so that I could watch Miss Marr and caught sight of Shirley Russell instead. If only she would notice me!

Shirley had about her the magic of a story. She and her brother Ian had come from England to stay with their aunt and uncle and be safe from the bombing. She had joined our class near the end of grade four. Shirley had a lovely voice, with an accent like the child movie actress Margaret O'Brien's. She also had golden ringlets, longer and fairer than Shirley Temple's. She was a War Guest. She was different, too, but everybody wanted to be her friend.

"Face front, Jean," Miss Marr said. "Here are your spelling words."

She had typed them for me on a big print typewriter. I bent over them, drawing each letter on the roof of my mouth with the tip of my tongue. I had discovered that this helped me to remember them. It also helped fill in time.

When the bell rang for recess, Miss Marr astonished me by saying to Shirley Russell, "This is Jean Little, Shirley. She can't see well. Would you be her friend and help her get into the right line when it's time to come back inside?"

*S*hirley smiled sweetly and nodded her golden head. I could not believe this was really happening. Shirley Russell was actually going to be my friend. At last I was going to have a girl to do things with, and not just any girl. The War Guest herself! We marched down the stairs and went out into the girls' side of the playground. I turned to Shirley, my smile shy, my heart singing.

Shirley scowled. Just under her breath, so that nobody but me could hear, she snarled, "You keep away from me. Get lost!"

Then she turned and ran.

"Be my partner, Shirley, and I'll give you my Crackerjack prize," I heard one girl call out.

There was a hubbub of offered bribes and vows of eternal friendship. Nobody looked in my direction.

I stood where I was, stunned into immobility. I should have guessed, perhaps, that our teacher had asked the impossible of the English girl. She was popular at the moment, but if she had me trailing after her, her accent might suddenly cease to be interesting and just be weird. She was a foreigner, after all, and she knew it.

Before any of them had time to notice me watching them, I walked away to the far side of the playground. I leaned up against a tall tree and stared off into the distance, as though I had my mind on things other than silly grade five girls. To keep myself from crying, I began talking to the tree that was supporting me.

"Are you lonely, too, tree?" I murmured. "If you are, I'll come every day and talk to you. We could be friends."

As I drew a shaking breath, much like a sob, I heard a gentle rustle above my head. I glanced up. The leafy branches seemed to nod to me.

You can count on a tree, I told myself. A tree is better than a person.

But I knew it was not true.

When we were supposed to line up to march in again, I heard Shirley's laugh and tagged on the end of the right line. I counted my steps on the way in. I'd find it tomorrow without any help from Shirley Russell.

Back at my desk, I heard Miss Marr ask two people to pass out pieces of paper. Staring down at the blank sheet, I hoped we were going to draw or write a composition.

"We're going to have a mental arithmetic test," Miss Marr said. "Write down the numbers 1 to 10 on your paper."

I bent my arm around my sheet, shielding it from

prying eyes, even though the others were not close to me.
I had a sinking feeling the test she was talking about
would involve those horrible times tables everybody but
me had mastered in grade three. I picked up the special
fat pencil Miss Marr had given me and did as I had been
told. As I waited for the first question, I clutched the
pencil so tightly that my knuckles whitened.

"Question one," said Miss Marr. "8 x 3."

I began to add. Eight and eight were . . . sixteen? Or
was it fourteen?

Three and three are six, I muttered inside my head,
changing my method of attack. I turned down two
fingers so that I would know when I reached eight.

"Question two," Miss Marr said. "6 x 4."

I gave up on question one and began to add fours. I
had reached twelve and four are sixteen when she went
on to question three.

When she reached question ten, I stared down at my
paper in dismay. All that was written on it were the
numbers 1 to 10 in a neat column. I had not managed to
get even one answer.

"Since this is the first day, you can each mark your
own paper," she said. "What is it, Ruth?"

"Can I sharpen my pencil?" Ruth Dayton's
voice asked.

"Yes. But hurry up. You are keeping us all waiting."

As she passed behind me, Ruth glanced over my
shoulder. I did not notice her small hiss of astonishment
as she took in the fact that I had not answered a single
question.

"The answer to question one is twenty-four," the

teacher said as Ruth regained her seat.

I knew that behind my back, forty pencils were checking the answer. I had to do something to look busy. With painstaking neatness, I pencilled in 24 beside the number 1.

"If you have 24 beside the number 1," said my new teacher, "check it right."

I stared down at my page. There, right next to the 1 was written 24. Feeling a little like a sleepwalker unable to stop herself, I put a check mark next to the answer my teacher had just dictated. After all, she had not said, "If you got the answer right . . ." She had said, "If you have the number 24 beside the number 1 . . ." And I did.

"The correct answer for Number 2 is also 24," she said then. I wrote that down.

"If you have the answer 24 beside the number 2, check it right."

We worked our way down the sheet. First she would tell us the answer. I would write it down. Then she would instruct us to "check it right," and I would put a neat check mark on the paper.

When the others had finished marking their answers right or wrong, Miss Marr said, "Raise your hand if you have ten answers checked right."

I looked at my arithmetic paper. There they were, all ten answers checked right. I raised my hand. As I did so, I expected something dramatic to happen, a thunderbolt to strike me dead or a huge voice to roar, *"Jean Little, what have you done?"* Nothing of the kind disturbed Miss Marr's classroom. The teacher looked around at the eight or nine raised hands.

"Good for you," she said.

I snatched my hand down and stared hard at a broken piece of chalk lying in the chalk trough. I did not check to see whether anybody admitted to having none checked right. I was sure I was the only one who would have missed them all.

As she began a geography lesson, I felt relief wash over me. Mental arithmetic was at an end, for that day, at least. Perhaps everything was going to be all right.

My happiness lasted until noon.

Ruth and Stella came marching up to my desk while I was putting away my books. They stared at me with contempt.

"I saw you," Ruth said.

"What a cheat!" Stella put in. Her eyes were gleaming.

"Saw me what?" I said feebly. "I don't know what you're talking about. I didn't cheat."

"You might as well save your breath," Stella sneered. "Ruth *saw* you and so did I. You copied down the answers after she said them out loud."

"Are you going to tell on me?" I heard, and despised, the bleat of panic in my voice. They had me at their mercy and we all knew it.

"Do you think we would tattle?" Stella said, as though such a thing had never been known to happen. "We won't tell."

I cheered up too soon. She had not finished.

"But if you don't tell her yourself what a cheater you are, nobody in this class will ever speak to you again. We don't intend to be friends with a cheater."

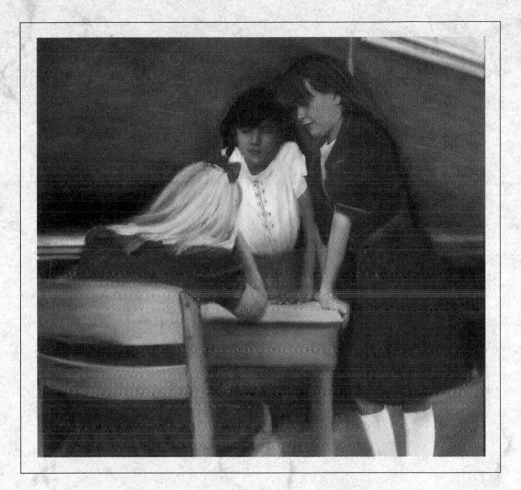

I had no choice. I longed for friends. In spite of
Shirley's snub, I still hoped that someday it might happen.
I couldn't risk turning the entire class against me.

Miss Marr was at her desk. I walked up to stand beside
it, moving slowly, trying hard to think of a way to confess

that would satisfy my class and not make Miss Marr
hate me.

Ruth and Stella lurked near enough to hear what I said.
I stood by my teacher's elbow until she looked up. Then
I took a deep breath and began. I stammered and
stuttered, but at last she took in what I was mumbling.
She told me to sit down. Then she waved Stella and
Ruth away.

"You two are supposed to be on your way home," she
said, her voice a little sharp. "Run along."

They went as slowly as they dared, but until they
were well out of earshot, Miss Marr ignored me.
She sharpened a pencil, then two. Finally she
turned and looked at me.

"I saw what you did, Jean," she said.

I gasped. Had she watched me cheat and said nothing?
I could not believe it.

She sat down near me and went on quietly.

"I don't think you meant to cheat, did you? It just
happened . . . when you could not get the answers fast
enough to keep up. Wasn't that the way it was?"

"Yes. That's just what happened," I told her, staring at
the floor and trying not to cry. "I'm no good at my
times tables . . ."

"You won't ever do it again, will you?"

I shook my head violently.

"Never ever!"

"Then we'll just forget it this time," she told me. "And
you'd better get busy learning your tables."

"I will," I promised. "Oh, I will."

I positively ran from the room. But when I got outside,

I found Ruth and Stella and four or five others waiting.

"What did she say?" they demanded.

I opened my mouth to tell them how nice Miss Marr had been. Then I stopped to think. The minute the other kids found out that I had not got the strap or been sent to the principal, they would all decide she was a "soft" teacher, easy to put one over on.

"I won't tell you," I said as bravely as I could, "but she was mad!"

Ruth seemed impressed. Stella gave me a scornful glance. But as she reached out to grab my hand and turn it palm up to see if it had strap marks on it, Jamie came around the corner of the school. He glanced in our direction, was about to go on, and then turned back.

"What's going on?" he demanded.

"He's my brother," I told them, feeling as though Robin Hood himself had come to my rescue.

The girls backed away.

"We're not hurting her," Ruth declared, but she was moving off step by step.

The rest melted away without a word. Jamie gave me an annoyed, big-brotherly look.

"You'd better hurry up or you'll be late for dinner," he said. "You can't walk with me."

I smiled. "I know," I told him humbly.

I knew better than to expect an eighth-grade boy to walk with a mere fifth-grade girl. Yet just knowing he was in the world, I felt protected all the way home.

Thinking About It

1. Are Jean Little's problems like everyone else's? Compare her problems with those of any other students in a classroom.

2. Be Miss Marr. Tell what went on in your classroom that made you decide not to punish Jean.

3. Step into Jean's classroom. Figure out what you can do to make a difference for Jean.

Me, aged 10, with my cat.

Another Book by Jean Little

Try *Mine for Keeps*, the story of a young girl's courage in the face of some pretty overwhelming challenges.

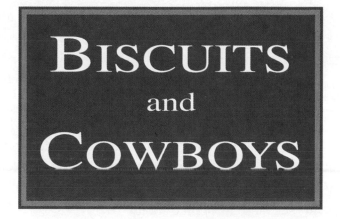

BISCUITS and COWBOYS

Justin's sisters think Justin has a lot of growing up to do. He and his friend Anthony call making a bed and cooking dinner "women's work" and refuse to help with either. Angry at his whole family, Justin goes off to visit his grandfather at his ranch and learns a little about what it means to get along with other people.

The sun beamed down and sweat rolled off Justin as he rode on with Grandpa, looking for broken wires in the fence. They were well away from the house, on the far side of the ranch. Flies buzzed around the horses and now gnats swarmed in clouds just above their heads. The prairie resounded

from *Justin and the Best Biscuits in the World*
by Mildred Pitts Walter

with songs of the bluebirds, the bobwhite quails, and the mockingbirds mimicking them all. The cardinal's song, as lovely as any, included a whistle.

Justin thought of Anthony and how Anthony whistled for Pepper, his dog.

It was well past noon and Justin was hungry. Soon they came upon a small, well-built shed, securely locked. Nearby was a small stream. Grandpa reined in his horse. When he and Justin dismounted, they hitched the horses, and unsaddled them.

"We'll have our lunch here," Grandpa said. Justin was surprised when Grandpa took black iron pots, other cooking utensils, and a table from the shed. Justin helped him remove some iron rods that Grandpa carefully placed over a shallow pit. These would hold the pots. Now Justin understood why Grandpa had brought uncooked food. They were going to cook outside.

First they collected twigs and cow dung. Grandpa called it cowchips. "These," Grandpa said, holding up a dried brown pad, "make the best fuel. Gather them up."

There were plenty of chips left from the cattle that had fed there in winter. Soon they had a hot fire.

Justin watched as Grandpa carefully washed his hands and then began to cook their lunch.

"When I was a boy about your age, I used to go with my father on short runs with cattle. We'd bring them down from the high country onto the plains."

"Did you stay out all night?"

"Sometimes. And that was the time I liked most. The cook often made for supper what I am going to make for lunch."

Grandpa put raisins into a pot with a little water and placed them over the fire. Justin was surprised when Grandpa put flour in a separate pan. He used his fist to make a hole right in the middle of the flour. In that hole he placed some shortening. Then he added water. With his long delicate fingers he mixed the flour, water, and shortening until he had a nice round mound of dough.

Soon smooth circles of biscuits sat in an iron skillet with a lid on top. Grandpa put the skillet on the fire with some of the red-hot chips scattered over the lid.

Justin was amazed. How could only those ingredients make good bread? But he said nothing as Grandpa put the chunks of smoked pork in a skillet and started them cooking. Soon the smell was so delicious, Justin could hardly wait.

Finally Grandpa suggested that Justin take the horses to drink at the stream. "Keep your eyes open and don't step on any snakes."

Justin knew that diamondback rattlers sometimes lurked around. They were dangerous. He must be careful. He watered Black first.

While watering Pal, he heard rustling in the grass. His heart pounded. He heard the noise again. He wanted to run, but was too afraid. He looked around carefully. There were two black eyes staring at him. He tried to pull Pal away from the water, but Pal refused to stop drinking. Then Justin saw the animal. It had a long tail like a rat's. But it was as big as a cat. Then he saw something crawling on its back. They were little babies, hanging on as the animal ran.

A mama opossum and her babies, he thought, and was no longer afraid.

By the time the horses were watered, lunch was ready. *"M-mm-m,"* Justin said as he reached for a plate. The biscuits were golden brown, yet fluffy inside. And the sizzling pork was now crisp. Never had he eaten stewed raisins before.

"Grandpa, I didn't know you could cook like this," Justin said when he had tasted the food. "I didn't know men could cook so good."

"Why, Justin, some of the best cooks in the world are men."

Justin remembered the egg on the floor and his rice burning. The look he gave Grandpa revealed his doubts.

"It's true," Grandpa said. "All the cooks on the cattle trail were men. In hotels and restaurants they call them chefs."

"How did you make these biscuits?"

"That's a secret. One day I'll let you make some."

"Were you a cowboy, Grandpa?"

"I'm still a cowboy."

"No, you're not."

"Yes, I am. I work with cattle, so I'm a cowboy."

"You know what I mean. The kind who rides bulls, broncobusters. That kind of cowboy."

"No, I'm not that kind. But I know some."

"Are they famous?"

"No, but I did meet a real famous Black cowboy once. When I was eight years old, my grandpa took me to meet his friend Bill Pickett. Bill Pickett was an old man then. He had a ranch in Oklahoma."

"Were there lots of Black cowboys?"

"Yes. Lots of them. They were hard workers, too. They busted broncos, branded calves, and drove cattle. My grandpa tamed wild mustangs."

"Bet they were famous."

"Oh, no. Some were. Bill Pickett created the sport of bulldogging. You'll see that at the rodeo. One cowboy named Williams taught Rough Rider Teddy Roosevelt how to break horses; and another one named Clay taught Will Rogers, the comedian, the art of roping." Grandpa offered Justin the last biscuit.

When they had finished their lunch they led the horses away from the shed to graze. As they watched the horses, Grandpa went on, "Now, there were some more very famous Black cowboys. Jessie Stahl. They say he was the best rider of wild horses in the West."

"How could he be? Nobody ever heard about him. I didn't."

"Oh, there're lots of famous Blacks you never hear or read about. You ever hear about Deadwood Dick?"

Justin laughed. "No."

"There's another one. His real name was Nat Love. He could outride, outshoot anyone. In Deadwood City in the Dakota Territory, he roped, tied, saddled, mounted, and rode a wild horse faster than anyone. Then in the shooting match, he hit the bull's-eye every time. The people named him Deadwood Dick right on the spot. Enough about cowboys, now. While the horses graze, let's clean up here and get back to our men's work."

Justin felt that Grandpa was still teasing him, the way he had in Justin's room when he had placed his hand on Justin's shoulder. There was still the sense of shame whenever the outburst about women's work and the tears were remembered.

As they cleaned the utensils and dishes, Justin asked, "Grandpa, you think housework is women's work?"

"Do you?" Grandpa asked quickly.

"I asked you first, Grandpa."

"I guess asking you that before I answer is unfair. No, I don't. Do you?"

"Well, it seems easier for them," Justin said as he splashed water all over, glad he was outside.

"Easier than for me?"

"Well, not for you, I guess, but for me, yeah."

"Could it be because you don't know how?"

"You mean like making the bed and folding the clothes."

"Yes." Grandpa stopped and looked at Justin. "Making the bed is easy now, isn't it? All work is that way. It doesn't matter who does the work, man or woman, when it needs to be done. What matters is that we try to learn how to do it the best we can in the most enjoyable way."

"I don't think I'll ever like housework," Justin said, drying a big iron pot.

"It's like any other kind of work. The better you do it, the easier it becomes, and we seem not to mind doing things that are easy."

With the cooking rods and all the utensils put away, they locked the shed and went for their horses.

"Now, I'm going to let you do the cinches again. You'll like that."

There's that teasing again, Justin thought. "Yeah.

That's a man's work," he said, and mounted Black.

"There are some good horsewomen. You'll see them at the rodeo." Grandpa mounted Pal. They went on their way, riding along silently, scanning the fence.

Finally Justin said, "I was just kidding, Grandpa." Then without planning to, he said, "I bet you don't like boys who cry like babies."

"Do I know any boys who cry like babies?"

"Aw, Grandpa, you saw me crying."

"Oh, I didn't think you were crying like a baby. In your room, you mean? We all cry sometime."

"You? Cry, Grandpa?"

"Sure."

They rode on, with Grandpa marking his map. Justin remained quiet, wondering what could make a man like Grandpa cry.

As if knowing Justin's thoughts, Grandpa said, "I remember crying when you were born."

"Why? Didn't you want me?"

"Oh, yes. You were the most beautiful baby. But, you see, your grandma, Beth, had just died. When I held you I was flooded with joy. Then I thought, *Grandma will never see this beautiful boy*. I cried."

The horses wading through the grass made the only sound in the silence. Then Grandpa said, "There's an old saying, son. 'The brave hide their fears, but share their tears.' Tears bathe the soul."

Justin looked at his grandpa. Their eyes caught. A warmth spread over Justin and he lowered his eyes. He wished he could tell his grandpa all he felt, how much he loved him.

THINKING ABOUT IT

1   Hop on a horse and ride along to the rodeo with
    Justin and Grandpa. Is there a little bit of cowboy
    in you? a lot? Would you rather see the rodeo
    or be in it?

2   Justin and Grandpa often talk about "men's work"
    and "women's work." What's that all about? Is
    there any difference?

3   Justin seems to be learning quite a bit from
    Grandpa. Think of an older person from whom you
    might learn something. What might you ask that
    person?

Grandchildren and Grandparents

Like Justin and his grandpa,
Ariel and her grandmother have
some good times together in
The Canada Geese Quilt by
Natalie Kinsey-Warnock. Find
out what role the quilt plays in
Ariel's life.

We Moved About a Week Ago

by Jack Prelutsky

We moved about a week ago,
it's nice here, I suppose,
the trouble is, I miss my friends,
like Beth, who bopped my nose,
and Jess, who liked to wrestle
and dump me in the dirt,
and Liz, who found a garter snake
and put it down my shirt.

I miss my friend Fernando,
he sometimes pulled my hair,
I miss his sister Sarah,
she shaved my teddy bear,
I miss the Trumble triplets
who dyed my sneakers blue,
and Gus, who broke my glider,
I guess I miss him too.

I really miss Melissa
who chased me up a tree,
I even miss "Gorilla" Brown
who used to sit on me,
the more I think about them,
the more it makes me sad,
I hope I make some friends here
as great as those I had.

F·74

BY EMILY CROFFORD

THE VALENTINE

My first thought when the new boy came into the classroom was that we girls had wasted a lot of time fussing with our hair. My second thought was that Miss Gibson hadn't been fair to us; she should have described him when she told us he would be coming.

"Class," Miss Gibson said, "this is Talmadge McLinn. His family has just moved here from eastern Tennessee." Neither her voice nor her expression threatened us, but her eyes, sweeping from one side of the room to the other, made it clear that we had better mind our manners.

"From Wild Hog Holler, to be exact," Talmadge said.

Maxine giggled and others sniggered. Miss Gibson glared at us and the sniggering faded out. I figured Maxine, who giggled about everything, was probably choking herself.

Talmadge's feet were so big, they called even more attention to his clubbed right foot. Clubfeet were not unusual, but I had never seen one like his. His weight came down on the outside of his little toe so that his heel was raised up about two inches from the floor even when he was standing still. He was wearing hightop work shoes—without socks, despite the January cold. His shabby overalls stopped before they reached the tops of his shoes. The other boys wore their best clothes, generally corduroy pants and blue shirts, to school.

Talmadge's hair, which reminded me of winter-dried grass, was longer than any I had ever seen on a boy. It hung down the back of his neck and hid the tops of his ears. His smile stretched from one side of his face to the other, offering all of us his friendship, asking for ours. I knew how he felt because I remembered how the kids had looked at me the first day I had come to this school. They had made such fun of my citified clothes— especially my neat new oxfords—that I had gone home and beat them with Daddy's tap hammer to make them look old. Like Talmadge, I had seemed foreign to the other kids. I glanced straight into his eyes, which were very blue, to let him know I sympathized with him.

"Which cheer ye want I should set in?" Talmadge asked Miss Gibson, and Stinky Sterret burst out laughing. Miss Gibson sent him out into the hall.

Stinky, I thought, had forgotten that when he had first come from Oklahoma the other boys had ragged him until he'd turned mean and earned the name Stinky.

At recess we girls talked about Talmadge. "I feel sorry for him," Josie said.

Maxine went into a fit of giggles. "But do you want him for a boyfriend?"

Josie tossed her head. "I have more boyfriends now than I know what to do with. I just said I feel sorry for him."

"Me too," I said. Since Josie and I were best friends, we practically always agreed with each other. "I don't think any of the boys will make friends with him—and Stinky is going to make his life miserable."

Stinky did too, beginning that very recess. He ran by Talmadge, grabbed his cap, and threw it to Raymond. Talmadge seemed to think it was a game and kept grinning and trying to recapture his cap while other boys joined in to keep it away from him. Some of the boys held the cap out to him and waited until Talmadge awkwardly reached them and held out his hand before tossing it to someone else. C. C. got a big laugh when he examined the inside of the cap, widened his eyes, and threw it quickly, shaking his fingers like the cap had lice in it.

We girls didn't think it was very funny, except for Maxine. We kept watching, though, waiting to see what would happen.

The smile on Talmadge's face held even when Stinky caught the cap, pinched it on his nose, and blew. That's when Miss Gibson, who had been standing close to the door talking to another teacher, stepped in. Walking fast, her head thrust forward like a snapping turtle's, she charged into the middle of the group, snatched the cap away from Stinky, and shoved him backward so hard he fell.

Maxine put her fist in her mouth.

You shouldn't have done that, Miss Gibson, I thought. From now on Stinky will make Talmadge his enemy.

Talmadge knew that too. Wiping his cap on the dead grass, he said, "Hit don't make no never mind." He settled the cap back on his head. "There now. Hit's good as new. They was just funnin', Miss Gibson."

Stinky might have been funning before. But now his mouth turned down at the corners in hate.

In class Talmadge grew quieter and quieter during the next two weeks. His hand stopped shooting up to answer

questions; he stayed in during recess and read rather than go outside.

John Edward, the boy I liked best, didn't act mean to Talmadge. He didn't seem to mind that Talmadge made a hundred in almost every test except arithmetic, either. It didn't surprise me. John Edward had never held it against me when I sat him down in spelling bees. One or the other of us had always been the last to go down until Talmadge came along. I couldn't understand how somebody who couldn't talk right could spell so well. Talmadge spelled both of us down two times out of every three.

While John Edward wasn't mean to Talmadge and talked to him, he didn't make friends with him. Nobody did. I stayed away from him too until Mother sent a note one day that I had had an earache the night before and couldn't go outside to play. At first Miss Gibson was in the room with Talmadge and me; then she left to go to the library. Her feet were still tapping down the hall when Talmadge, carrying the book he was reading, came up to a desk in the next row from mine and sidled into it.

"I'm sorry ye're feeling porely, Meg," he said.

"Oh, I'm all right," I said. "I had an earache last night. It's gone except for a twinge now and then."

"My sister gits earaches too," he said. "They must be awful." He looked so concerned he made me fidget.

"Ye ever read this here book?" he asked me.

I glanced at the door and listened hard to see if any of the kids were hanging around in the hall. The only sounds were the muted squeals and laughter from the school grounds.

"I don't think so," I said, and turned my head to the side to read the title. *Bob, Son of Battle*, it said. There was a picture of a collie dog's face under the title. "Is it about a dog that fights a lot?"

Talmadge chuckled as if the question pleased him. "That there word Battle throws ye, don't it? Hit did me too. Battle was the name of the dog's daddy. A gray dog—sheep dog—he was."

"Oh," I said.

Talmadge turned from his place at about the middle of the book to the front pages and handed the book over to me.

"See, that's whar ye start cotching on—where they compare Bob with Rex, Son of Rally."

I silently read the paragraph he pointed to:

"Ay, the Gray Dogs, bless 'em!" the old man was saying. "Yo canna beat 'em not nohow. Known 'em ony time this sixty year, I have, and niver knew a bad un yet. Not as I say, mind ye, as any on 'em cooms up to Rex son o' Rally. Ah, he was a one, was Rex! We's never won Cup since his day."

I handed the book to Talmadge. "It's hard to read."

"At first it is," he said, "but ye'd soon git the hang of it. I ain't never lent it out before, but ye kin borry it when I'm done this time." He turned some pages and read aloud,

> *"Did yo' feyther beat yo' last night?" she inquired in a low voice, and there was a shade of anxiety in the soft brown eyes.*
>
> *"Nay," the boy answered; "he was a goin' to, but he niver did. Drunk," he added in explanation.*

It sounded like music when Talmadge read it. "You talk kind of like them," I said.

He nodded. "The Thorntons—my mother was a Thornton—come from the Dalelands like them." He turned sideways in the desk and leaned toward me, his hands folded between his knees. "Dalesmen air from England," he explained. "My dad's people was from across the border—in Scotland. Fer back the Thorntons and the McLinns spilt blood feudin' one with t'other. So when my mother and father got married, neither side would have aught to do with them. Mother used to cry a lot about it. The feudin' ain't never quit, albeit my father says cain't any two people tell the same tale about why it commenced in the first place."

"Oh," I said. I didn't know what else to say. It seemed so important to him that I added, "They were mean to treat your mother and father that way."

Talmadge sat up straight again and stroked the book with his fingertips. "I got this here book fer Christmas when I was but a tyke. I'm just now gittin' to the point I can read it good." After a pause, he said, "I'm glad my father don't beat me like David's does in the book. My dad's not a drunk neither."

I knew why he told me that. As if it were some awful scandal, Maxine had informed us that his father made corn whiskey out on the uncleared land where Talmadge's family lived. I wondered if he helped his father make moonshine, but it wouldn't be polite to ask. Besides, there was something I wanted to know more.

"Talmadge—aren't you going to fight him?"

He didn't pretend he didn't know whom I was talking about. A week ago, in front of the whole class, Stinky had challenged Talmadge to come behind the ditchbank and fight. Since then Stinky and the three boys who hung around with him had made remarks about Talmadge being yellow.

Talmadge closed the book and shook his head. "We come here to git away from fightin' much as to make a livin'. I seen enough fightin' to last me a lifetime. We'uns just want to live peaceable." He traced his finger around the picture of the dog's face on the front of the book. "I've took a vow not to never fight agin." Glancing at me, he said, "I ain't told nobody else except John Edward."

"I won't tell," I said. "John Edward won't either."

The bell rang; I grabbed my science book and pretended to be studying. Talmadge started back toward his desk. Too late. Maxine was standing in the doorway, her bird eyes darting from one of us to the other. She and her best friend Bonnie Lou walked by my desk and, as if she were speaking privately to Maxine, but loud enough for others coming in to hear, Bonnie Lou said, "Look's like Meg has a new sweetheart." Maxine bent over from the waist, she giggled so hard.

For the rest of the day they and some of the other girls wrote notes to each other about Talmadge and me. I managed to ignore them, which I knew worked best, but sometimes it was hard. I kept wishing John Edward would give me the new whistling ring he had brought to school and shown around that morning. Everybody knew Bonnie Lou spent half her time writing his name in her notebook.

When the last bell rang I quickly gathered my books. Most of the time when the weather was nice I went the long way home, around by the post office and the store, so I could be with Josie. Today, though, I intended to walk the short, direct way home with Grace Bowers. Grace lived on the other side of me on the Blue Road. She never tarried on the schoolground, so I had to hurry. I was about to put my coat on when Miss Gibson said, "Meg."

"Yes, ma'am."

"How do you feel?"

"Fine," I said.

"Good. You evidently forgot that this is your day to empty the wastebasket."

I worked my way through the crowded hall, emptied the wastebasket into the big trash can, and ran back. Ignoring the people still in the room, I put on my coat and scarf and pulled my cap down over my ears.

Talmadge, wearing an overcoat that came almost to his

ankles and made him look like a scarecrow dressed for
winter, came over to me.

"Ye look right dauncy, Meggie," he said.

I could feel my cheeks turn pink. Several boys,
including Stinky, were in a huddle at the back of
the room, and I had an uneasy feeling that it had
something to do with Talmadge. The last thing I
wanted was for them to think there was any truth in
what Bonnie Lou and Maxine had been saying about my
liking Talmadge.

"I've got to hurry," I said, and scooted out the door.

Before I had reached the road, much less caught up
with Grace, I sensed excitement behind me, turned to
look, and found myself going back. I didn't like
fistfights—my stomach had already tightened up—but
something seemed to pull me to watch.

I saw immediately what had happened. Stinky had
come up behind Talmadge and yanked his *Bob, Son of
Battle* book out of his hand. For the first time since he
had started to our school, all of the meekness went out
of Talmadge.

"Give it back," he said, his voice so commanding that
it took Stinky by surprise.

Talmadge was taller than Stinky, but he had the bad
foot. In addition, Stinky could make his biceps muscle
jump when he bent his arm at the elbow and knotted his
fist. He showed off that way a lot. Most of the boys were
afraid of him. When he had finally turned on them for

tormenting him about being an Okie, he had won three fights in one afternoon. I didn't figure Talmadge had much of a chance.

Talmadge held out his hand for the book. For a minute Stinky looked like he was going to give it back to him, but the other boys were nudging him, saying things like, "Git him, Stinky!" "Go on." "Make him show his yellow streak."

John Edward didn't do that, but he didn't make a move to stop it like he had other times either. He licked his lips, glancing from Stinky to Talmadge.

Stinky dropped the book and kicked it to the side. "You want it, hillbilly, pick it up!" he said.

A tremor passed through Talmadge, but because of our conversation at morning recess I realized that it didn't come from fear. It came from fighting within himself. It struck me that John Edward knew that too.

In one move, like a mother wildcat I had seen spring at a dog who had come too close to her cubs, Talmadge shucked his coat, took a step forward, and hit Stinky high on the jaw. Stinky staggered and the people watching gasped with surprise. Stinky recovered quickly, though, lowered his head, and charged, swinging hard. Talmadge moved in a circle, ducking and swaying to dodge Stinky's fists. Even when Stinky's blows landed, they

were short or glancing. Talmadge didn't move his
head back enough once, though, and his nose began to
dribble blood.

Kids from other classes were there now too, some
silent, some shouting to stop it, others egging them on.
The smell of nervous sweat from all the bodies made me
feel like I was going to throw up. But I stayed, even
shoved people aside who tried to get in front of me.

Talmadge had only thrown one punch, but suddenly
his fist shot out again. He hit Stinky in the same place on
his jaw. Stinky went down. Talmadge took a couple of
long awkward steps and straddled him, pinning his

shoulders to the ground. He had won!

And then Talmadge did a terrible thing. He started to cry. Holding his arm over his eyes and his bleeding nose, he got up off of Stinky, picked up his book, and walked away.

Some of the crowd, led by Stinky's friends, were shouting, "Go back to Wild Hog Holler!" I took a few steps toward Talmadge. You did the right thing, I wanted to tell him. You had to stand up for yourself.

The kids were all staring at me. "Go back to Wild Hog Holler!" I yelled just once before I ran—toward the Blue Road and home.

Generally a fight was the topic of conversation the next day, but nobody mentioned the one between Talmadge and Stinky. It was like we all wanted to forget what had happened. I kept thinking about John Edward, who was known as a peacemaker, and the way he had licked his lips when Talmadge and Stinky were about to fight. I finally worked it out. He hadn't been excited about the possibility of their fighting, but about whether or not Talmadge could stick to his vow. I decided I liked another boy, Tom Garrity, better than I did John Edward.

I didn't want to talk with Talmadge after that day, though. He was too different; he didn't belong. John Edward looked through him. Nobody included him, or bothered him. He had become an outcast. When I knew he was looking at me, I pretended to be busy with my school work. When he walked beside me as we were leaving the building, I answered him politely and hurried away as soon as I could.

"It's just politeness, that's all it is," I explained to Grace as we were walking home in a cold drizzling rain. "Mother and Daddy have drummed being polite and kind into me since I was born, so I can't help it."

Grace didn't answer. This was one of her silent days. I jabbered about other things, about Miss Gibson and Josie's new haircut and Bonnie Lou's spitefulness. We had walked another quarter of a mile before Grace said, "Meg, you ain't being honest. You really like Talmadge."

"I don't like him! I can't stand him!"

Grace shrugged and said nothing more.

Finally I broke the silence. "You know good and well that if I showed that I liked him, the other kids would peck me raw."

Grace still didn't say anything, just looked at me with sad, old eyes.

I couldn't be mean to Grace, though, even when she treated me like I was a silly little kid. She had befriended me before anybody else at school had accepted me. And I knew about her life at home. She had to tend the babies and scrub floors and wash clothes when she wasn't chopping and picking cotton. I had seen the bruises on her back from her father's razor strop. So at my house, I just said, "See you tomorrow."

She nodded and walked on, her head bent against the icy drizzle. I knew I didn't have to worry about Grace telling anyone that I had admitted I liked Talmadge. I didn't tell her secrets to other people, not even to Josie, and she didn't tell mine.

With Valentine's Day coming up, I began to get especially nervous about Talmadge. If he brought me a mushy valentine I would just die.

Miss Gibson tried to skip having a valentine box altogether, but we argued so well she gave in. "It's the only fun thing we have between Christmas and the end-of-school plays," Maxine said. "After all," Josie added, "this is the last year. From seventh grade up we can't have a valentine box." "It's a tradition," Peggy explained in her sighing, tired voice.

Miss Gibson picked Peggy, a girl everybody liked okay but didn't choose as best friend, to make the valentine box.

Mother had never liked valentine boxes, not even for first grade, much less sixth. Considering that, I should have known better than to fuss about having to make my own valentines.

"All the kids who live up on the highway get theirs in town," I told her.

"With money so scarce, that must be a sacrifice," she said.

F·92

I grumbled under my breath and she turned on me. "You can either make them from the wallpaper book or forget it. And if you make one, you have to make them for every person in the class."

The next morning I hesitated before approaching the box, considering holding out Stinky's and Bonnie Lou's and Maxine's and Talmadge's. Peggy had made a pretty last box. She had wrapped it in white crepe paper and pasted red composition-paper hearts of different sizes all over it. Oh, what the heck, I decided. I might as well end it by giving a valentine to everybody. I dropped all my envelopes through the slot.

Miss Gibson didn't hand out the valentines until the last period, and by that time I was a wreck. I had started imagining that I would only get four or five, believing that nobody really liked me. I got thirteen. Peggy and Josie and John Edward got more, but I didn't feel too bad. The one from Tom Garrity was store-bought with an elephant on the front. "I've got a trunkful of love for you, Valentine," it said. And between the valentine and the inside of the envelope nestled a stick of Doublemint chewing gum. I couldn't wait to show Bonnie Lou and Maxine. Neither of them had given me a valentine.

I felt sorry for Talmadge and was glad I had made a valentine for him. Mine had been one of the three he received. I had just printed "Happy Valentine's Day" in red and signed my name. There was no way the kids could make something of that, I thought.

Talmadge did though. He caught up with me on the front steps as we were leaving school.

"Shore makes a feller feel good to git a valentine from a blossom-eyed gal like you, Meg," he said. "I hope hit don't fret ye that I didn't give you one. I didn't give nary one—couldn't git around to making any."

"That's all right," I said quickly and, turning my back to him, started talking to Peggy.

At home I dropped my valentines in my top dresser drawer for keepsakes. I had put them and Valentine's Day and the valentine box out of my mind by the next day.

When we woke up Saturday morning, Daddy said, "I think it's going to snow." Bill and Correy and I prayed that it would, and after it finally started in mid-afternoon, we prayed that it would stick. It kept melting as fast as it hit the ground, though, and I got too cold to play outside anymore. Besides, the ground had gotten sticky wet.

Mother said I could help her quilt if I worked slowly and carefully. I pulled a stool up to the quilting frame. Outside the wind moaned softly around the corners of the house, but in the front room where we were quilting the heater glowed pink on its sides. The house smelled of burning wood and the gingerbread Mother had baked.

Cozy and happy, I didn't even look up when Brownie gave a warning growl from the front porch. Daddy came up behind me and ducked down to peer past my shoulder out the window. At that moment I heard a call: "Hello!" My head jerked up. There, beside the road, stood Talmadge. He was wearing the ugly long coat and his cap—and somebody had cut his hair. It looked awful, like it had been chopped off with his cap as a guideline.

I slid off the stool, and one of those miserable burning blushes I couldn't do a thing about raced from my neck right up to my hairline.

"It's the new boy in our class," I said. "Talmadge."

Daddy went to the door, his face crinkling with amusement at my embarrassment, which made it worse.

"Come on in," Daddy called as warmly as if Talmadge were Mr. Limon, the plantation owner.

Talmadge came over the footbridge, scraped the blue-tinged mud off his shoes on the front steps, took his cap off and stuffed it in his right pocket, and came inside, nodding and smiling. His nose was red and his eyes were teared from the cold.

"This is Talmadge," I said stiffly. "He moved here from Tennessee."

"From Wild Hog Holler, to be exact," Talmadge said, smiling all over his face.

Mother smiled back at him. Daddy chuckled with a merriment that matched Talmadge's.

"I know your father," Daddy said. "Fine man. Go on over by the heater and get warm, Talmadge."

Talmadge held his hands to the heater a minute, then turned his back to it. His nose had started to drip. He wiggled his hand into his overcoat pocket, took out a white rag, and blew his nose.

"Take Talmadge's coat for him, Meg," Mother said. There was a puzzled note in her voice, as if she didn't understand why I seemed to have forgotten the art of making welcome.

"I believe I'll keep it on awhile," Talmadge said. "I'm chilled clear to the marrow."

Bill and Correy came bursting in through the kitchen from the back yard, puffing and laughing.

"Talmadge!" Bill exclaimed, "What're you doing here?"

"Hi, Bill," Talmadge said.

It didn't surprise me that Bill knew Talmadge—kids in the lower grades often knew the ones above them. It did surprise me that Talmadge knew Bill.

Correy was staring at Talmadge's clubfoot. Mother should teach him not to do that, I thought. It isn't polite.

"That's Correy," Bill and I said at the same time, his tone proud and cheerful, mine forced. Talmadge squatted down, one knee up, one down, man fashion, so he would be eye-level with Correy.

"Hi, Correy." He pointed at his foot. "Hit were like that when I come into this world." Standing up, he winked at Correy. "Don't slow me down none, though."

Then he walked straight over to me, to the spot where I stood like an upright board, reached into his left overcoat pocket, took out a big white envelope, and handed it to me.

"I hitched into town this morning and bought this," he said.

Fumbling, I opened the envelope.

"Hit's a valentine," Talmadge said. "Since Valentine's Day has done passed, I got it for half price. With money I saved up myself."

The valentine was beautiful, lacy with delicate flowers and hearts on the front. Inside it said, "To My Sweetheart."

"I was goin' to git one that said 'To My Friend,'" Talmadge said nervously, "but they didn't have none like that."

With his bad foot he had walked miles in bitter weather to bring a valentine to me. It made my throat ache. As I continued to gaze silently at the valentine, I could tell that he was waiting for me to say something. Mother and Daddy and Bill and Correy were waiting too, waiting for me to thank Talmadge and ask him to stay and have gingerbread and buttermilk with us.

I relaxed. If the kids at school found out about Talmadge bringing the valentine, I would laugh and say, "I thought I would die!"

"It's the prettiest valentine I ever saw," I said. "Thank you very much."

Talmadge's naked ears turned red. He put his hands in

his pockets and rocked back and forth, beaming like he heard a song playing in his head.

Smiling, I asked, "Would you like to have some gingerbread and buttermilk with us?"

"Shore is a temptation," Talmadge said, "but I've got to git on home. Been gone so long I 'spect my mother's as worrified as a tabbycat what's lost one a' her kits."

"At least take a piece with you," Mother said. She went quickly into the kitchen and came back with a big square of the cake.

We watched out the window as Talmadge started up the road eating gingerbread. The snow had almost fizzled out, and the sun was sparkling around the edges of broken clouds.

"I'm proud of you," Daddy said to me in a soft, pleased voice. "Proud that you choose your friends according to what's inside them. I've heard about the way the lad's been shunned."

I stared down at the floor, too ashamed to lift my head. I could see Talmadge sitting hunched at his desk, his eyes pleading with me to be his friend; I could hear myself shouting, "Go back to Wild Hog Holler!"

"It took courage not to go along with the crowd," Daddy said and reached out to touch me.

"Don't—please." My words came out sounding choked.

I hurried into my room and scrambled into my coat, then ran blindly outside to the barn and climbed up to the loft. The fragrant, loose hay gave under my weight, bouncing back up behind me as I crawled across it, cradling me when I sank down into it, muffling the sound when I said, "Talmadge, I'm sorry," and let the tears burst free.

THINKING ABOUT IT

1   Who has the problem in this story—Talmadge or the others in school? What is the problem? What would you do to help solve it?

2   Why does Meg yell "Go back to Wild Hog Holler!" at Talmadge? Does she mean it?

3   Many stories don't really end. You get to imagine what happens afterward. What do you imagine happens afterward in this story?

Stories from the Blue Road
"The Valentine" isn't the only good story in this book by Emily Crofford. Check it out!

Little Green

Men

by Barry B. Longyear

Jhanni caught his breath and rested
in the shade of a boulder; he
had found nothing. His father had
forbidden him to search with
the other Star Scouts for the UFO
reported three days ago, and he
wouldn't think of disobeying his
father. Still, I said nothing
about searching on my own,
thought Jhanni.

"All this about 'invaders from
outer space' is nonsense." His
father had been unshakable on the
subject, and nearly everybody
thought the same way since the
probe to Venus had reported no
detectable life on the planet.
Adventurer 7 had met with a
mishap on its way to Saturn, and
Jhanni's father had been furious.
"More taxpayers' money thrown
away on foolishness! We should
spend the money to take care of

problems here." Evidently the government felt the same way. When Jhanni turned thirteen the space program was canceled. Along with the program, the Star Scouts were officially scrapped.

Still, Jhanni's friends, and Star Scouts from all over, kept their squadrons alive to search for evidence—proof that would rekindle the space program and put them back on their road to the stars. Every time a UFO was reported, the squadron in that area would turn out and search for evidence—disturbed soil, burn marks, abandoned equipment—anything. But two years of searching had turned up nothing.

"Someday," Jhanni had told his squadron, "someday we'll find the proof we need, but until then we have to keep on trying." Nevertheless, one by one, the Star Scouts were leaving the squadron. Some, like Jhanni, were forbidden to waste good study time on such foolishness; others were discouraged; and still more had come to believe as their parents believed: Space travel costs too much to spend for uncertain returns. Jhanni's father had pulled him out of the squadron when his grades began to drop.

"We've had UFO reports for years. Spaceships, death rays and little green men from outer space, and it's always been something that could be explained. I don't want you ruining your education by wasting your time with it."

Jhanni loved his father, but he had argued with him for

the first time in his life. "How do you know there's no
life on other planets? Isn't it possible?"

"No one knows for sure, Jhanni, but I'll tell you this:
Before I believe it, someone's going to have to show me
one of those little green men."

And that's what we're looking for, thought Jhanni, one

of those little green men. He pushed away from the boulder and stepped into the sunlight. Shielding his eyes, he looked around. The squadron was searching the hills north of the development where the "object" was reported to have come down during the dust storm three days ago. His father wouldn't give his permission to join the search in the hills, and Jhanni was so angry it took him three tries to properly cycle the airlock on his home before stepping out into the desert.

He went south from the development to search the boulder field, although the "object" was reported north. The wind storm was blowing south that day, thought Jhanni. It's possible; not probable, but possible.

As he looked out over the boulder-strewn desert floor, the evening shadows grew long. Soon it would be dark and the desert cold. He checked the light buckle and heater in his belt and headed for his favorite boulder. At every turn he strained to glimpse the spaceship he hoped would be there. He knew he could get a better view from his boulder, the largest one in the field. It was pockmarked with great holes bored there by the action of the wind and sand, and Jhanni hadn't been there since he was a child playing with the friends who later became his mates in the Star Scouts.

Sometimes he would take one of his mother's blankets and some extra power cells and spend most of an icy night on his boulder, looking at the stars and dreaming of traveling among them. But the dreams became fewer as he grew older. There was no official interest anymore in moons, planets, stars or anything else that might cost the taxpayers more money.

As the sun dropped below the horizon, the stars appeared, and Jhanni watched them as he reached his boulder and climbed to the top. As he watched the countless pinpricks of light from unknown and unexplored stars, he let himself dream again of flying among them. His eyes glistened and he looked down. Maybe it is childish, he thought. The road to the stars is closed unless people can see the little green man in the flesh. And maybe . . . maybe the little green men don't exist after all.

Jhanni thought he heard a sound, and he looked over his shoulder. Seeing nothing unusual, he crawled over and around the boulder, looking into the tiny, wind-blown caves. There was nothing. He shrugged and stood atop the boulder, looking toward the development and his home. The outside light was on at his house, and his mother would scold him if he were late for dinner. He shook his head when he remembered he still had a tough stretch of homework to do and a math test in the morning. He knew he'd better pass this one. Too much imagination and not enough perspiration, his father would say if he failed. Taking one last look at the stars, Jhanni sighed and began to climb down from the boulder.

PING.

Jhanni froze. Slowly he turned his head in the direction of the sound. Deep in the shadow of a wind hole, a tiny light danced back and forth. Warily he crept toward the hole.

"HEY!"

Jhanni picked himself off the ground, knocked there by the suddenness of the sound. He reached to his belt and turned on his light buckle, aiming it at the hole. Inside there was a small, white cylinder propped up on spindly legs supported by round pads. The cylinder was dented, and its legs looked bent and battered.

"Turn off the light! I can't see."

Jhanni turned off his light buckle, and as his widening eyes adjusted again to the dark, tiny lights on the cylinder appeared and illuminated the hole. On one side of the object a tiny door opened, and a small, white-clad creature emerged, looked around and climbed down a tiny built-in ladder to the bottom of the wind hole. Jhanni peered closely as the creature lifted something and aimed it in Jhanni's direction.

"Can you hear me?"

"Uh . . ."

"Hold it." The creature adjusted a knob on its chest. "Had to lower the volume a bit. Good thing you dropped by; I only have a day's life support left."

"Uh . . ." Jhanni tried to untie his tongue, a million questions in his mind competing for the first answer. "Are you . . . are you from up there?" He pointed up. "How can you talk to me, and where . . .?"

"One thing at a time. That's where I come from, and I'm talking to you through a universal translator. I rigged it up with a speaker from the lander console in case anyone came by."

"What happened?"

The creature threw up its tiny arms. "What didn't? I've been out of touch with my base ever since the wind blew me into this hole three days ago, damaging my oxygen regulator and radio. I'm running a little short. Can you get me to an oxygen-enriched atmosphere?"

"Well . . . there's my gas box. I raise tropical insects, and they're oxygen absorbing. I did it for a school

F·108

project in biochem once, and . . ."

"Do the bugs eat meat?"

"Oh. Well, I can put them in another container. Can you fly or anything? My home's quite a walk from here."

"I guess you better carry me, but take it easy."

"I will." Jhanni picked up the little creature and held it in his hand, surprised at its weight. It was only as tall as one of Jhanni's fingers. He could just barely see the creature shaking his head inside his tiny helmet.

"I can't get over how big you Martians are. Wait until Houston hears about this!"

Jhanni laughed. "If you think I'm big, wait until you see my father!" And wait until my father gets a load of you, thought Jhanni. "By the way, creature, what color are you under that suit?"

"My name's Frank Gambino, Captain, United States Air Force. I'm sort of brown; why?"

"No special reason." Jhanni slipped the tiny creature into his pocket and began climbing down from the boulder. The little man isn't green, thought Jhanni, but he'll do. As he reached the desert floor and started to run home, he stopped himself just in time from patting his pocket.

JUST SUPPOSE...

by Eve Bunting

When I began writing for young people I was given some advice: write what you know!

The advice was good, but it boxed me in. I wanted to write about everything, and I certainly don't know everything. And then I made a wonderful discovery. What you don't  know you can learn. That discovery set me free.

I'd never written science fiction books for young people, so trying to do one was a happy challenge. *Day of the Earthlings* began, as so many stories begin, with a "suppose."

Some people suspect there is life on other planets. Suppose they are right? Suppose there are Martians on Mars who don't want Earthlings to know they exist. And suppose, just suppose, there is one Earth boy there, living with them. How did he get there? Did he like it? Or did he long to be back on Earth with others of his own kind?

I had the first ingredients for a story. Now I needed to find out everything I could about Mars. At my library I checked out all the scientific magazines. I read *The Martian Chronicles,* a book by Ray Bradbury. I went to the California Institute of Technology and to the Jet Propulsion Laboratory. The scientists there were happy to answer my questions and add a few theories of their own.

"Suppose a race of people does live on Mars. How would they look?" I asked.

"They would probably be small because they would have to have adapted to the strong winds that blow on the planet. They might walk bent over. I'd guess they would have underground cities to escape the cold."

"I plan to have an Earth boy there," I said. "Would this be possible?"

They looked astonished.

"It's a story," I reminded them.

"Well, his lungs would have to be changed. Earth lungs breathe mostly oxygen. On Mars he would breathe carbon dioxide."

I took frantic notes. "What would his new world look like?"

"Rocky. Dry. Water would be scarce. They would probably have to bring it from a Polar ice cap."

I asked and asked and they answered. I was ready.

The story I wrote about Cort, the Earthling, is his adventure. But it is also the adventure of two Earth explorers who come on a perilous journey. It is a story of a life and death choice, there on the sinking, swallowing sands of the great desert of Nerre. And of a boy who understands for the first time his truest values.

"Why do we look for other worlds?" the space explorer asks as he lands on another planet. Without hesitation he answers himself: "Because we must always reach for new knowledge."

Indeed we must. I hope you will enjoy reading the story.

DAY OF

THE EARTHLINGS

by Eve Bunting

When Cort was six or seven, he
realized that he was not like the
other Martians.

"Why am I so much bigger
than all my friends?" he asked
his father.

"Because you are an Earthling,
my son. We Martians are small
so that we are well adapted to
our wind and our cold and our
life underground."

"Is it because I am an Earthling
that my eyes are such a
strange shape?"

"Yes," his father said.

"Tell me about Earth and how
I got here," Cort asked, and his
father told him.

"We on Mars are a very advanced people. We took our spaceships to Earth and to Moon and to Saturn before other worlds dreamed of such things. One of our space travelers brought you back once, a long time ago. It was wrong. He should not have done such a thing; but it was done, and we made the best of it."

"Were the people angry with him?"

"They were. Such a terrible thing has never happened again." He reached to touch Cort's hair. "Your mother and I had no children. We took you, and we have loved you always."

"I know," Cort said.

"Do you remember the operations?" his father asked. "Your lungs were Earth lungs and needed oxygen. Our doctors adjusted your body to carbon dioxide. Do you remember it at all, Cort?"

"I don't think so," Cort said slowly.

et, somewhere, far far back in time there was a cloud that spun, and a voice crying, and pain. There must be memories, or else why was there in him this hunger for something he didn't have and didn't know?

The hunger grew with the years. Sometimes at night it would waken him. Sometimes at night, he'd come up to the shining cold of the Martian surface, and he'd look into the blackness where the planet Earth lay. That was where he'd been born. The pull of it was as strong as

gravity inside him and as strange. He was fifteen years
old, and he'd never seen an Earthling; but now the
Earthlings were coming.

Cort's father knew what Earth was like. He'd been
there twice on a spaceship. He'd taught himself the Earth
language by monitoring the space stations, and Cort had
learned it from him.

"The sky there is blue, not black like ours," his
father said. "They have great wide seas and water that
runs in rivers such as we had billions of years ago.

In their houses water flows from pipes, and they use it without thought."

That was perhaps the strangest thing of all. Here on Mars water was life and as precious. It was brought from the Polar ice caps by ice-gathering machines or mined underground from the permafrost.

"Their wind does not blow night and day with the strength of ours, and it is warmer there. The Earth men live above ground."

"It sounds . . . it sounds nice." Cort heard the little catch in his voice, and he turned his face from his father.

"It is," his father said. "It should be enough for any people; but the Earthlings would like to take over Mars, too."

"If they come, we could fight them off," Cort said; and he wondered at the falseness of his words. When he spoke of "they" what did he mean? He was one of "them," wasn't he? "We" and "They." How could he separate the two?

Now the Earthlings were coming.

Cosmos 21, their space station, reported Patriot I on its way from Earth. Its touchdown would be on the plain of Nerre.

Nine times already the Earth men had sent their spaceships to Mars in search of life. They had never found it, but this time was more dangerous. This time human men would land to search the Martian planet.

"If they find nothing on this trip, perhaps they will look to Saturn or Venus and leave us alone," Cort's father said; "and since they've chosen Nerre for the touchdown . . ." He left the sentence unfinished and smiled.

Nerre was a desert and as empty as the Earth's Sahara. The closest Martian underground city was more than two hundred kilometers away. None of their ice-gathering machines worked that zone, and it held none of their telescopes or space antennae. It was good that that was the chosen spot.

A Martian crew travelled to Nerre. In two hours they constructed an underground dugout from which they could watch, unseen. Cort was one of the crew.

When the work was finished, he stood beside his father on the bare plain of Nerre and looked into the day blackness of the sky.

The sun shone through its ice halo, but he saw it speckled by a dust dazzle of blowing sand.

Tomorrow Patriot I would come through that shimmer of sand, it would land, and its doors would open, and . . . Cort's heart beat fast. Cosmos 21 reported two Earth men on the Lander. Soon, soon they would be here.

———

Ellis Carver huddled in Patriot I's Lander as it rushed toward Mars. He could see Jonty Johnson's face through the glass of his helmet. The face was lettuce green. He hoped Jonty wasn't going to throw up. He hoped their

F·118

touchdown would be easy. He hoped they'd live through it.

Sweat rolled down his face, and there was no way to get a finger under his helmet to scratch the itch. It was better to think about the itch than to think about the touchdown.

It had taken eight years and more than a billion dollars to get Patriot I off the ground. So far everything had gone perfectly. They'd cruised 900 miles above Mars taking pictures. Whatever happened now, that part of the mission had been a success. The pictures had already been beamed back to earth.

Whatever happened now! The words echoed in his mind and seemed to bounce off his space helmet. All they needed was one big rock, and the Lander would topple. Suppose . . . no, don't suppose.

He'd been training for four years, ever since he was eighteen. "Reacts well under stress." That's what his very first NASA report had said. Ellis licked his lips. He tried to catch the sweat trickle with his tongue. Reacts well under stress. It wasn't that he was scared. It was just that everything was unknown and so much depended on them.

There was a loud, plopping noise—the rocket engines firing, bringing them on a downward path. That soft, swishing sound was their parachute unfurling. Six miles an hour—that's what their speed should be now. The red light flashed on the control panel. Thirty seconds till touchdown. Why did they call it a control panel? They didn't have control of a darn thing. Everything was pre-programmed. They were on a computer course with no way to change it.

The light blinked and blinked. Twenty-seven, twenty-six. Ellis watched the flashing red eye as it ticked away the seconds.

Each of the Martian crew men had a telescopic periscope. It was reed-thin, crafted to be almost invisible from ground level. Their dugout was five kilometers from the touchdown zone.

Cort watched the small ship coming silver through the black dust-dazzle of the sky. Above it the detached parachute hung wispy as a cloud. The three landing legs were down, and a shower of sparks shot from the ship's side.

"The braking rockets," his father muttered.

Slowly, delicately the Lander eased down. One foot pad touched Martian ground. The wind gusted, and the metal trembled. Then the other two feet took hold, and the craft swayed and settled. Cort held his breath. His heart-sound was loud in his ears. Soon he would have his first glimpse of Earthlings—his own kind, his very own. Soon now.

———————

Inside the Lander, Ellis and Jonty Johnson carried out their first tasks. Ellis relayed their safe touchdown to the orbiting mother ship. Jonty used the remote scoop to pick up soil samples and store them in the thermal vault. The Lander's camera moved down below the ship to photograph the foot pads and the ground around them. The high television camera on top of the craft activated and began rolling. It was time to leave the Lander. But whatever happened now, this much had been accomplished. Whatever happened now!

Jonty swung the side hatch up and let down the runway. His wave to Ellis said, "You first."

Ellis stood by the side of one of the small mobile Rovers and looked through the dust at the Red Planet. It wasn't red. He felt awe and a sense of something of tremendous importance. His eyes were seeing what no human eyes had seen before.

Ahead of him lay desert, more lifeless than anything on earth. No shrub grew—no plant. There was only a broad, barren plain, the wind whipping its rocky sand knee high, flinging it against the Lander as if sensing an alien object. In the distance he could see a rim of sharp-edged craters. Ellis drew a deep breath. They'd been lucky. Suppose they'd tried to land there?

Mars! He said the word under his breath. For this second he was Columbus on the deck of the Santa Maria, seeing the New World for the first time.

Jonty tapped his shoulder, and Ellis nodded. He checked his air tanks and tubes. Then he climbed behind the Rover's wheel, his body awkward in his heat-controlled suit. The sound of the Rover's engines was lost in the whine of the wind. His headlights gilded the dust that snapped through the air. Slowly the Rover rolled on its tractor treads down the runway.

He would travel due North; Jonty due South. Tonight they'd re-charge their air tanks and refuel the Rovers. Tomorrow they'd head East and West. The Rover's control panel would buzz at the return point. When the buzzer sounded, half the air and half the fuel was gone. There was a half volume reserve tank.

Ellis sat in the Rover at the foot of the Lander and looked up at it. It was like a great silver beetle on a rock, a dragonfly maybe. Its searchlight shone reassuringly from above, giving light for the television camera—light for them too, a hope in the dark to look back to. Ellis took a shivery breath. Air wasting. Time to start. The strange stone desert stretched ahead and to either side. From time to time he stopped to gather and store a strange, glittering rock, a blackened, burned-out lump of stone. From time to time he checked his space compass. There was no sign of life, but Ellis felt no disappointment. He knew now that he had not expected to find any. "Why do we climb mountains?" he asked himself.

"Because they are there."

"Why do we look for other worlds?"

"Because we must always reach for new knowledge." He looked back at the Lander, and it was a beacon that would guide him home.

The Rover rolled slowly up to one of the craters. Ellis stopped it. What had caused this round, black hole? A meteor, crashing into Mars billions of years ago? An ancient volcano? He should have a soil sample. He got out of the Rover and stepped close to the crater's rim. Then suddenly, unbelievably he wasn't standing on rock; he was standing on sand. Then he was standing on nothing, and he was falling, tumbling into what looked like a grey snow drift below.

———

Cort saw the Earth man fall. His periscope brought everything close enough to touch, and Cort had been watching hungrily. He wanted to press his face close to the window on that space helmet. He wanted to see Earth eyes, to touch Earth skin; and then the Earth man fell.

Cort heard the gasps, the faint hissing of breath as the Martians realized what had happened. His father raised his periscope to get a down-view into the crater.

"He can't get up," he said sadly.

Cort wound his periscope high. The Earthling lay face down on top of the powder sand. Somehow he had sense not to struggle. With the weight of his tanks and thermal suit, to struggle would be to sink and suffocate.

Cort wet his lips and looked at his father.

"What will we do?"

His father's eyes held the same sadness as his voice. "There is nothing we can do. To help him we would have to reveal ourselves. Perhaps the other Earth man will come to his rescue." He spoke so softly that Cort could scarcely hear him. "Perhaps he'll be in time."

Cort swallowed. "How much air does he have?"

"I see the red light on his Rover. The warning buzzer is on. One Earth hour left. Perhaps a half hour emergency oxygen, no more."

Cort looked at the stranded Earthling one more time and could bear to look no longer. "You taught me that life is precious," he told his father. His anger burned inside him. "Is an Earth life not precious?"

"It is," his father said. "But we must count the cost."

Cort sat by himself and tried to understand his

feelings. The pull
was back, drawing
him strongly,
surely toward the
Earth man. Leave
him to die? How could
they do that? And yet . . .
and yet . . . Cort chewed at
his underlip till he felt the sting
of blood.

The other Martians watched intently through their
periscopes. No one saw Cort take the coil of woven rope
and slip away.

Ellis listened to the Rover's buzzer and made his time
calculations. Then he accepted the fact that he was going
to die.

The shock of the rope dropping over his shoulders
made him flounder and sink several inches.

"Don't move," a voice said.

Ellis' heart fluttered wildly. Jonty. . . it must be Jonty!
Cautiously he raised his head.

What? Who?

A boy stood at the crater's rim holding the end of the
rope. "Slowly. Put it under your arms," the boy said in
halting English.

Ellis got his arms through the loop and held on to the

rope with all his strength. He felt dazed, in some sort of shock where he knew this was happening and knew too that it couldn't be.

"Good." The boy wore Eskimo clothes of some glowing fabric, but that was a human face under the hood and that was a human voice. There was a drop of dried blood on the boy's lower lip.

The boy stepped back out of sight, and Ellis panicked and moved. He felt himself sink. "Hey," he called; but his word was hollow inside his helmet. Then he heard the Rover's motor start, and the rope under his arms tightened. He was dragged like a big fish through the sand drift and up the edge of the crater. On level ground he lay gasping, too stunned to move as the boy wrapped the rope round and around him, trussing him like a chicken.

"I will let you go," the boy said. "But first you must give me your word. No one is to know that you saw me. No one is to know what happened. Do you give me your word as an Earth man?"

Ellis looked at the face so close to his own. A human, breathing Martian air, living here. It couldn't be. It couldn't.

"Promise!" The boy tugged savagely at the binding ropes. "Promise, or I will throw you back in."

Ellis managed to move his head in a nod. He mouthed, "I promise." Reacts well under stress, the report had said. Reacts well.

"You saw nothing. You got yourself out." The voice was fierce. The human face was pressed close against his helmet window. Their eyes met and held.

"Who are you?" Ellis begged silently. "How are you here?"

Shadows like clouds moved behind the boy's eyes. To Ellis it seemed as though he stared at him forever. The boy raised his hand and gently touched the side of Ellis' helmet. Then he unwound the rope, bunched it loosely, and edged back.

Ellis struggled to his knees. He held on to the side of the Rover and pulled himself up. The boy had disappeared. Should he try to follow him through the speckled dark? Which way had he gone? Had there been a boy at all? There must have been. Someone, something had dragged him from death.

Ellis shook his head. For a few seconds he stared into the emptiness; then he climbed behind the Rover's wheel and turned it toward the light of the Lander.

His mind was a jumble of unanswered questions. He'd promised . . . What had he promised? But this was the cosmic discovery of all time, and he was a scientist. Nothing should stand in the way of this truth.

It could be that they wouldn't believe him. It sure wasn't easy to believe. And he'd promised the boy. Ellis thought of the boy's eyes, the way he'd touched his helmet as if saying goodbye.

Now he was under the Lander. He looked up at it and remembered what he'd forgotten, and he knew that the decision wasn't his to make.

———

Cort leaned against the outside wall of the dugout. He had disobeyed his father and gone against the will of his people. The race across the rocky ground was like a dream now, the running so fast that there had been no time to think. The Earth man's face, so like his own and yet so different! For a second, as he'd looked down at that face, his mind had been filled with impossible thoughts. He could ask the

Earthling to take him back with him. The operations could be reversed. He'd be with his own people. He'd leave Mars forever. He'd looked down, and there had been a moment of choice, and for the first time he'd known what that choice was. *These* were his people. He belonged here with the known things, with the acceptance, with the love. There was a sadness in finally knowing who he was, and a relief too.

Now his hands trembled as he pushed open the door. His father and the others must have seen him through their periscopes as he ran to help the Earth man. They hadn't tried to stop him. There was some hope in realizing that.

They faced him as he stood against the door, and he saw at once that there was no anger. But there was something else.

"He won't tell," Cort said shakily. "He gave me his word as an Earth man."

The room held silence, and something else.

Cort spoke to his father, "I had to go."

"I know," his father said. "But there was one thing you

F•131

didn't know, my son, or didn't remember." He spread out his hands. "We saw you running; and we could have brought you back, but it was already too late. The Lander has a television camera with a dark-view eye. You are there, my son, on film. The pictures must already be on their way back to Earth."

Someone pulled down his periscope, and the click of it was the only sound in the room.

"It will take them many years to build another spaceship," his father said, "but nothing will stop them now. We will leave here, move to the opposite side of our planet, but they will find us."

"What have I done?" Cort heard his voice rising out of control.

"Not you alone," his father said. "What happened tonight was started many years ago when you were brought here. The fault is also ours."

There was the crackle of static. Cosmos 21.

They froze, listening.

The words that came from the box were slurred with excitement, but no one in the room failed to understand.

"Patriot I reports life found on Mars," the space voice said. "Repeat. Patriot I reports life found on Mars."

PULLING IT ALL TOGETHER

1   As you read *Day of the Earthlings,* what surprised
    you? What did you wonder about? If the story
    were true, what would happen eventually?

2   The characters in *Ask Me Again Tomorrow* have
    decided to get together on a panel and give advice
    about growing and changing. Think about several
    characters. What advice would each give?

3   Some books need more pages. Suppose *Ask Me
    Again Tomorrow* had more. You're in charge. Figure
    out a story you would add to finish the book. It can
    be one you have read or one you wish you could
    read. Describe it.

More Science Fiction
When a UFO lands in Nick's backyard, Elise
wonders what the aliens want. You can find out
in Beatrice Gormley's book, *Wanted: UFO*.

Arthur, For the Very First Time
by Patricia MacLachlan
Harper, 1980
Arthur takes notes on what happens around him, but nothing ever seems to happen to him. Then he spends an unforgettable summer with his aunt and uncle.

Max and Me and the Wild West
by Gery Greer and Bob Ruddick
Harper, 1988
You step into some old contraption and before you know it, you travel back in time one hundred years. And from what you can figure, you're in big trouble.

A Rat's Tale
by Tor Seidler
Farrar, Straus & Giroux, 1986
Montague Mad-Rat isn't an ordinary rodent. He's got big dreams and high hopes. His story is a remarkable one.

A Wrinkle in Time
by Madeleine L'Engle
Orchard Books, 1989
All Meg wants to do is find her father. Little does she know that this will mean taking off on an adventure through space and time.

by Mildred Pitts Walter

Mariah Keeps Cool
by Mildred Pitts Walter
Bradbury Press, 1990
Big sisters are not easy to live with, especially if yours just arrived and thinks she doesn't need to follow rules. That's just the beginning of Mariah's problems.

Pueblo Boy: Growing Up in Two Worlds
by Marcia Keegan
Dutton, 1991
Timmy, a ten-year-old Pueblo Indian, really does have the best of both worlds. At school he uses a computer and plays baseball in the yard; at home he learns the customs and prayers of his ancestors. This beautiful photoessay is one you'll want to share.

Born to Dance SAMBA
by Miriam Cohen
Harper, 1984
Maria Antonia is certain that she'll become Queen of the Samba. Imagine her surprise when she discovers that her friend is an even better dancer than she is.

Aekyung's Dream
by Min Paek
Children's Book Press, 1988
Aekyung speaks only Korean, but everybody else speaks English. Even the birds seem to sing in English. Will she ever feel at home again?

LITERARY TERMS

Style

Style is the writer's way of telling the story. Authors make many decisions as they write: What should the tone be? Which words convey the theme? Should there be imagery? poetic language? sound devices? These decisions affect the style of the writing. The poet Jack Prelutsky wants to make you laugh with "We Moved About a Week Ago." His style creates a light hearted, humorous effect: "I even miss 'Gorilla' Brown/ who used to sit on me."

Autobiography

An **autobiography** is the story of a real person's life written by that person. In "Memories of Fifth Grade," Jean Little tells of her life when she was in the fifth grade. An auto-biography is written from the first-person point of view.

Characterization

A well-developed character will often change in behavior from beginning to end of the story. That change in behavior is a way of showing **characterization.** Meg, in "The Valentine," is afraid to be friendly toward Talmadge at the beginning of the story. At the end, she has grown up enough so that she is able to show her friendship.

Imagery

Imagery helps us understand how things look, sound, smell, taste, or feel. In "The Valentine," the author uses imagery to describe the characters. Meg says of Talmadge that "his hair reminded me of winter-dried grass." Later she describes Talmadge as "smiling all over his face." These pieces of imagery help us picture what Talmadge is like.

Plot

The **plot** of a story often develops from conflict between two characters. In "The Valentine," the conflict between Talmadge and the other students causes him to prove what kind of person he is. Conflict within a person also influences plot. Meg struggles within herself, knowing she wants to be a friend to Talmadge but she's afraid of what others will think. The author includes several episodes in which Meg tries to decide how to behave toward Talmadge.

Science Fiction

A **science fiction** story (like fantasy) is a story that could not really happen. Science fiction tells about life in the future, often using known scientific details. In a science fiction story you'll usually find a great many machines and inventions that we can only dream about now. "Little Green Men" and *Day of the Earthlings* are both examples of science fiction.

Simile

A **simile** is a comparison of two things that are not really alike. In a simile, the author uses the words *like* or *as* to make a connection between the two unlike things. A simile can make a character description more interesting. The author of "The Valentine" uses similes to give a stronger picture of some of the characters. She describes Talmadge as looking "like a scarecrow dressed for winter." In another place, she describes Miss Gibson as walking fast, "her head thrust forward like a snapping turtle's."

Vocabulary from your selections

a dapt (ə dapt′), **1** make fit or suitable; adjust: *Can you adapt your way of working to the new job?* **2** change so as to make suitable for a different use: *The story was adapted for the movies from a novel by Jane Austen.* *v.* —**a dapt′er, a dap′tor,** *n.*

ad mit (ad mit′), **1** say (something) is real or true; acknowledge: *She admits now that she made a mistake. His opponent had to admit defeat.* **2** allow to enter; let in: *He was admitted to a trade school. Windows admit light and air.* **3** have room for; be large enough for: *This garage door will admit two cars abreast.* *v.,* **ad mit ted, ad mit ting.**

ath lete (ath′lēt′), person trained in exercises of physical strength, speed, and skill. Baseball players, runners, boxers, and swimmers are athletes. *n.* [*Athlete* is from Latin *athleta,* and can be traced back to Greek *athlon,* meaning "a prize, a contest."]

athlete

at mo sphere (at′mə sfir), **1** air that surrounds the earth. **2** mass of gases that surrounds, or may surround, any heavenly body: *the cloudy atmosphere of Venus.* **3** air in any given place: *the damp atmosphere of a cellar.* **4** general character or mood of one's surroundings; surrounding influence: *a religious atmosphere, an atmosphere of excitement.* **5** unit of pressure equal to 14.7 pounds per square inch (1.03 kilograms per square centimeter). *n.*

charge (chärj), **1** ask as a price; demand payment: *The grocer charged 75 cents a dozen for eggs. This store charges for delivery.* **2** price asked for or put on something: *The charge for delivery is $3.* **3** put down as a debt to be paid: *We charged the table, so the store will send a bill for it.* **4** a debt to be paid: *Taxes are a charge on property.* **5** load or fill: *charge a gun with powder and shot.* **6** give an accumulation of electricity, which may be discharged, to: *charge a battery.* **7** amount needed to load or fill something. A gun is fired by exploding the charge of powder and shot. **8** an accumulation of electricity in a battery, condenser, etc., which may be discharged. **9** give a task, duty, or responsibility to: *My parents charged me to take good care of the baby.* **10** task; duty; responsibility: *I accepted the charge to take good care of the baby.* **11** care; management: *Doctors and nurses have charge of* *sick people.* **12** person or thing under the care or management of someone: *Sick people are the charges of doctors and nurses.* **13** give an order or command to; direct: *She charged us to keep the plan secret. The judge charged the jury to come to a fair decision.* **14** an order; command; direction: *a judge's charge to the jury to arrive at a verdict.* **15** accuse: *The driver was charged with speeding.* **16** accusation: *He admitted the truth of the charge and paid a fine.* **17** rush with force; attack: *A herd of elephants charged the hunters. The captain gave the order to charge.* **18** an attack: *The charge drove the enemy back.* 1,3,5,6,9,13,15,17 *v.*, **charged, charg ing;** 2,4,7,8,10-12,14,16,18 *n.* —**charge′less,** *adj.*

charge off, 1 subtract as a loss: *The store owner charged off all unpaid debts over three years old.* **2** put down as belonging: *A bad mistake must be charged off to experience.*

in charge, having the care or management: *The mate is in charge when the captain leaves the boat.*

in charge of, having the care or management of: *My sister-in-law is in charge of the book department of the store.*

charge (definition 17)

a hat	**i** it	**oi** oil	**ch** child	**ə** stands for:
ā age	**ī** ice	**ou** out	**ng** long	a in about
ä far	**o** hot	**u** cup	**sh** she	e in taken
e let	**ō** open	**ù** put	**th** thin	i in pencil
ē equal	**ô** order	**ü** rule	**ŦH** then	o in lemon
ėr term			**zh** measure	u in circus

cruise (krüz), **1** sail about from place to place on pleasure or business; sail over or about: *We cruised to Bermuda on our vacation. Freighters and tankers cruise the oceans of the world. The coast guard cruised along the shore.* **2** a voyage from place to place for pleasure: *We went for a cruise on the Great Lakes last summer.* **3** to travel or journey from place to place: *The taxicab cruised the city streets in search of passengers.* **4** to travel in a car, airplane, boat, etc., at the speed at which it operates best. 1,3,4 *v.*, **cruised, cruis ing;** 2 *n.* [*Cruise* comes from Dutch *kruisen,* meaning "to cross, cruise," and can be traced back to Latin *crux,* meaning "a cross."]

de spise (di spīz′), look down on; feel contempt for; scorn: *They were despised for their dishonesty.* *v.,* **de spised, de spis ing.** —**de spis′er,** *n.*

de tect (di tekt′), find out; discover; catch: *I detected my friends hiding in the bushes. Can you detect any odor in the room?* *v.* [*Detect* comes from Latin *detectum,* meaning "uncovered."]

de tect a ble or **de tect i ble** (di tek′tə bəl), capable of being detected. *adj.*

dis may (dis mā′), **1** sudden loss of courage because of fear of danger: *They were filled with dismay when they saw the rattlesnake.* **2** trouble greatly; make afraid: *The thought that she might fail the test dismayed her.* 1 *n.,* 2 *v.* —**dis may′ing ly,** *adv.*

dis o bey (dis′ə bā′), refuse to obey; fail to obey: *The student who disobeyed the teacher was punished.* *v.*

dramatic

dra mat ic (drə mat′ik), **1** of drama; having to do with plays: *a dramatic actor.* **2** seeming like a play; full of action or feeling; exciting: *the dramatic reunion of a family separated during wartime.* **3** striking; impressive: *a dramatic use of color. adj.* —**dra mat′i cal ly,** *adv.*

for bid (fər bid′), not allow; say one must not do; make a rule against; prohibit: *The teacher forebade running in the halls. v.,* **for bade** or **for bad, for bid den** or **for bid, for bid ding.**
for bid den (fər bid′n), **1** not allowed; against the law or rules: *Eve ate the forbidden fruit.* **2** a past participle of **forbid.** *My parents have forbidden me to swim in that river.* 1 *adj.,* 2 *v.*

gore¹ (gôr), blood that is shed; thick blood; clotted blood: *The battlefield was covered with gore. n.*
gore² (gôr), wound with a horn or tusk: *The angry bull gored the farmer in the leg. v.,* **gored, gor ing.**
gore³ (gôr), **1** a long, three-sided piece of cloth put or made in a skirt, sail, etc., to give greater width or change the shape. **2** put or make a gore in. 1 *n.,* 2 *v.,* **gored, gor ing.**

grav i ty (grav′ə tē), **1** the natural force that causes objects to move or tend to move toward the center of the earth. Gravity causes objects to have weight. **2** the natural force that makes objects move or tend to move toward each other; gravitation. **3** heaviness; weight: *He balanced the long pole at its center of gravity.* **4** seriousness; earnestness: *The gravity of her expression told us that the news was bad.* **5** serious or critical character; importance: *The gravity of the situation was greatly increased by threats of war. n., pl.* **grav i ties.**

hilarious

hi lar i ous (hə ler′ē əs *or* hə lar′ē əs), very merry; very funny; noisy and cheerful: *a hilarious tale, a hilarious party. adj.* —**hi lar′i ous ly,** *adv.* —**hi lar′i ous ness,** *n.*

in gre di ent (in grē′dē ənt), one of the parts of a mixture: *The ingredients of a cake usually include eggs, sugar, flour, and flavoring. n.* [*Ingredient* comes from Latin *ingredientem,* meaning "a going into."]
in vade (in vād′), **1** enter with force or as an enemy; attack: *Soldiers invaded the country to conquer it. Grasshoppers invade fields and eat the crops.* **2** enter as if to take possession: *Tourists invaded the city.* **3** interfere with; break in on; violate: *The law punishes people who invade the rights of others. v.,* **in vad ed, in vad ing.** —**in vad′er,** *n.*

mat a dor (mat′ə dôr), the chief performer in a bullfight who kills the bull with a sword. *n.*

meek (mēk), **1** not easily angered; mild; patient. **2** submitting tamely when ordered about or injured by others; too shy or humbled; yielding: *Don't be meek about asking for a promotion. adj.* —**meek′ly,** *adv.* —**meek′ness,** *n.*

meth od (meth′əd), **1** way of doing something: *a method of teaching music. Roasting is one method of cooking meat.* **2** order or system in getting things done or in thinking: *If you used more method, you wouldn't waste so much time. n.* —**meth′od less,** *adj.*

mis hap (mis′hap), an unlucky accident: *By some mishap the letter went astray. n.*

mishap

mis sion (mish′ən), **1** a sending or being sent on some special work; errand. An operation by one or more aircraft against the enemy is called a mission. **2** group sent on some special business: *She was one of a mission sent by our government to France.* **3** group of persons sent by a religious organization into other parts of the world to spread its beliefs. **4 missions,** *pl.* an organized effort by a religious group to set up churches, schools, hospitals, etc.: *foreign missions.* **5** business on which a mission is sent: *carry out a mission.* **6** station or headquarters of a religious mission. **7** business or purpose in life; calling: *It seemed to*

a hat	i it	oi oil	ch child	ə stands for:
ā age	ī ice	ou out	ng long	a in about
ä far	o hot	u cup	sh she	e in taken
e let	ō open	ù put	th thin	i in pencil
ē equal	ô order	ü rule	ŦH then	o in lemon
ėr term			zh measure	u in circus

be her mission to help improve living conditions in the city. n. [Mission is from Latin missionem, which comes from mittere, meaning "to send."]

out cast (out′kast′), **1** person or animal cast out from home and friends: *The criminal was an outcast of society.* **2** being an outcast; homeless; friendless. **1** *n.,* **2** *adj.*

pan to mime (pan′tə mīm), **1** a play without words, in which the actors express themselves by gestures. **2** gestures without words. **3** express by gestures. **1,2** *n.,* **3** *v.,* **pan to mimed, pan to mim ing.**

pantomime

per i scope (per′ə skōp), instrument that allows those in a submarine or trench to obtain a view of the surface. It is a tube with an arrangement of prisms or mirrors that reflect light rays down the tube. *n.*

re lieve (ri lēv′), **1** make less; make easier; reduce the pain or trouble of: *Aspirin will relieve a headache. We telephoned to relieve our parents' uneasiness.* **2** set free: *Your coming relieves me of the job of writing a long letter.* **3** free (a person on duty) by taking his or her place. **4** bring aid to; help: *Food and medicine were sent to relieve the flood victims.* **5** give variety or a pleasing change to: *The new red couch will relieve the drabness of the room.* *v.,* **re lieved, re liev ing.**
—**re liev′a ble,** *adj.*

sac ri fice (sak′rə fīs), **1** act of offering to a god. **2** the thing offered: *The ancient Hebrews killed animals on the altars as sacrifices to God.* **3** give or offer to a god: *They sacrificed oxen, sheep, and doves.* **4** a giving up of one thing for another: *Our teacher does not approve of any sacrifice of studies to sports.* **5** give up: *sacrifice one's life for another, sacrifice business for pleasure.* **6** loss from selling something below its value: *They sold their house at a sacrifice because they needed the money.* **7** sell at a loss. **8** (in baseball) a bunt that helps a base runner to advance, or a fly that allows a base runner to score, although the batter is put out. 1,2,4,6,8 *n.,* 3,5,7 *v.,* **sac ri ficed, sac ri fic ing.** —**sac′ri fic′er,** *n.*

short en ing (shôrt′n ing), **1** butter, lard, or other fat, used to make pastry, cake, etc., crisp or crumbly. **2** act of a person or thing that shortens. *n.*

skil let (skil′it), a shallow pan with a long handle, used for frying. *n.*

skillet

strand¹ (strand), **1** leave in a helpless position: *She was stranded a thousand miles from home with no money.* **2** run aground; drive on the shore: *The ship was stranded on the rocks.* **3** shore; land bordering a sea, lake, or river. 1,2 *v.,* 3 *n.*

stranded

strand² (strand), **1** one of the threads, strings, or wires that are twisted together to make a rope or cable. **2** thread or string: *a strand of pearls, a strand of hair. n.*

swerve (swèrv), **1** turn aside: *The car swerved sharply to avoid hitting the truck. Nothing could swerve her from reaching her goal.* **2** a turning aside: *The swerve of the ball made it hard to hit.* 1 *v.,* **swerved, swerv ing;** 2 *n.*

a hat	i it	oi oil	ch child	ə stands for:
ā age	ī ice	ou out	ng long	a in about
ä far	o hot	u cup	sh she	e in taken
e let	ō open	u̇ put	th thin	i in pencil
ē equal	ô order	ü rule	ᴛʜ then	o in lemon
ėr term			zh measure	u in circus

vow (vou), **1** a solemn promise: *a vow of secrecy, marriage vows.* **2** a promise made to God: *a nun's vows.* **3** make a vow: *I vowed never to leave home again.* **4** make a vow to do, give, get, etc.: *vow revenge.* 1,2 *n.,* 3,4 *v.* —**vow′er,** *n.* —**vow′less,** *adj.*

talent

marriage **vows**

tal ent (tal′ənt), **1** a special natural ability: *She has a talent for music.* **2** person or persons with talent: *That young singer is a real talent.* **3** an ancient unit of weight or money, varying with time and place. *n.*

u ten sil (yü ten′səl), **1** container or implement used for practical purposes. Pots and pans are kitchen utensils. **2** instrument or tool used for some special purpose. Pens and pencils are writing utensils. *n.*

utensils

ACKNOWLEDGMENTS

Text

Page 6: "La Bamba" from *Baseball in April and Other Stories,* copyright © 1990 by Gary Soto, reprinted by permission of Harcourt Brace Jovanovich, Inc.

Page 6: Lyrics from "La Bamba" by Ritchie Valens. Copyright © 1958 by *Picture Our Music* (renewed). All rights administered by Windswept Pacific. All Rights Reserved. Used by permission.

Page 20: *El Chino* by Allen Say. Copyright © 1990 by Allen Say. Jacket art copyright © 1990 by Allen Say. Reprinted by permission of Houghton Mifflin Company.

Page 40: "A Dream in Bright Sunlight," by Allen Say. Copyright © 1991 by Allen Say.

Page 44: "Writers" from *Hey World, Here I Am!* by Jean Little. Text copyright © 1986 by Jean Little. Reprinted by permission of HarperCollins Publishers.

Page 46: "Memories of Fifth Grade" from *Little by Little* by Jean Little. Copyright © 1987 by Jean Little. Reprinted by permission of Penguin Books Canada Limited.

Page 63: "Biscuits and Cowboys" from *Justin and the Best Biscuits in the World* by Mildred Pitts Walter. Text copyright © 1986 by Mildred Pitts Walter. Reprinted by permission of Lothrop, Lee & Shepard Books, a division of William Morrow & Company.

Page 72: "We Moved About a Week Ago" from *Something BIG Has Been Here,* poems by Jack Prelutsky, drawings by James Stevenson. Text copyright © 1990 by Jack Prelutsky. Illustrations copyright © 1990 by James Stevenson. Reprinted by permission of the Publisher, Greenwillow Books, a division of William Morrow & Company.

Page 74: "The Valentine" from *Stories from the Blue Road* by Emily Crofford, copyright © 1982. Used by permission of Carolrhoda Books, Inc., 241 First Avenue North, Minneapolis, MN 55401.

Page 100: "Little Green Men" by Barry B. Longyear from *Spaceships & Spells* edited by Jane Yolen, Martin H. Greenberg & Charles G. Waugh. Copyright © 1987 by Jane Yolen, Martin H. Greenberg and Charles G. Waugh. Reprinted by permission of HarperCollins Publishers.

Page 110: "Just Suppose . . . " by Eve Bunting. Copyright © 1991 by Eve Bunting.

Page 112: *Day of the Earthlings* by Eve Bunting. Published by Creative Education, Inc. Reprinted by permission of the author.

Artists

Illustrations owned and copyrighted by the illustrator.
Javier Romero, 6–19
Allen Say, 20–39
Lee Christiansen, 44–45
Hilary Mosberg, 46, 50, 53, 57, 58
Anna Rich, 62, 66, 69
James Stevenson, 73
Anthony Russo, 74–99
John Kleber, 100–101, 103, 106, 108
Tim Jonke, 112–132

Freelance Photography

Pages 46-58: Hilary Mosberg
Photographs not listed were shot by ScottForesman.

Photographs

Page 40: Photo of Allen Say courtesy of Richard Allen
Page 61: Courtesy of Penguin Books Canada Ltd.
Page 110: Courtesy of Eve Bunting
Page 138: Courtesy Gary Cranham/Rapho/Foto Researchers
Page 139: Courtesy Charles G. Summer
Page 140R: Courtesy Arthur Tilley/FFG
Page 142B: Courtesy Nova Scotia Information Service
Page 143R: Courtesy Billy E. Barnes/Stock Boston

Glossary

The contents of the Glossary entries in this book have been adapted from *Intermediate Dictionary,* Copyright © 1988 Scott, Foresman and Company, and *Advanced Dictionary,* Copyright © 1988 Scott, Foresman and Company.